WHAT PEOPLE ARE SAYING

The King's Bridal Company is an honest view of the incredible destiny of the Lord's bride, and the qualifications necessary to participate in this magnificent end-of-the-age reality. The Lord is preparing a people without spot or wrinkle. In the pages of this book, you will find an honest and forthright portrayal of the process necessary for the bride of Christ to emerge with intimacy and power. This book is filled with biblical affirmations and prophetic insight to help people be equipped and anointed for their purpose. I love the way Sal incorporates personal encounters with the Holy Spirit with biblical truth to affirm this reality. I thoroughly enjoyed this book, and believe it will be a great help to those experiencing the awakening of a bridal call and the deep desire to enter into union with the Messiah.
— **Paul Keith Davis**
WhiteDove Ministries

Sal Cerra clearly understands the end-time bridal company. The insight that he has, due to the many visions and visitations from the Lord, and his pin-point scripture references, gives you a solid base of the accuracy in this book. Jesus is looking for laid-down lovers who will express His desires and His heart, but we understand that not all will represent Him in this way. Sal's book gives us the perfect image of what Jesus is looking for in His bride. This book is a must-read for anyone who wants to be part of that select company when Christ returns for His adorned.
— **Apostle Joseph Dowell**
Fountain of Love Ministries, Phoenix, New York

Sometimes in life you meet someone who is truly a different individual. Sal Cerra is one of those people. He is different because of His intense love for Jesus and is a sincere lover of God. Sal operates within the principles of the Holy Spirit that allows him to escape the traps of legalism. He is funny, joyful, focused, and playful with all the qualities of an anti-Pharisee. He is absorbed with a passion for Jesus

and radiates that passion when he writes and speaks. We need more men like Sal to lead us into a fuller love relationship with Jesus! It's my honor to know the man who captures the heart of Jesus in his everyday walk.
— **Scott Fitzsimmons**
Prophetic Minister

The King's Bridal Company is a timely book for the end-time generation of believers—a company that has responded to the challenging call to make itself ready. Through this book, Sal encourages the reader to take a good look at oneself and discover that we are often not who we appear to be. Sal shares his own experiences with insecurities and apprehensions before having encounters with Jesus. He emboldens us to stand and begin to walk even while we are in the midst of a crooked and perverse generation. There are three non-negotiables that this book conveys to inspire us to be ready: Developing *intimacy* with Jesus in the Secret Place; *Purity*—Matthew 5:8 tells us that the pure in heart get to see God, and purity has us staying clean in a dirty world; and t*he fear of the Lord*—having a continual awareness of Him, a deep reverence for Him, and sincere commitment to obey Him. *The King's Bridal Company* is for those who want their reflection to be of Him.
—Aaron Evans
President, The Emerging Daniel Company, Int'l

Salvatore Cerra has given us a glimpse of the bride of Christ from a perspective of the Holy of Holies, looking out rather than looking in. Sal is a man of great character and integrity who spends every possible moment with the Groom in worship and adoration. It's during these intense times of intimacy when he is caught away in the Spirit to experience life-changing encounters in order to come back and relay these heavenly visions, provoking us to seek His face, not just His hand. I highly recommend this incredible book as I would the humble author.
— **Pastor Jarvis Ovalles**
Ovalles Ministries

There are few people I have met who have such passion and devotion to the Lord and His kingdom as Sal Cerra. In his new book, *The King's Bridal Company*, Sal reveals the longing heart of the Lover of our Souls to just spend time with us—His bride. The real-life supernatural experiences Sal shares throughout the book are both compelling and convicting. I highly recommend this book to those who are seeking a more intimate relationship with the Lord and want a glimpse into the supernatural realm.
— **Cathy Sanders**
Worship Leader, Author, Founder and Owner of CS Book Design

THE KING'S *Bridal Company*

Reflections of a King

SAL CERRA

The King's Bridal Company: Reflections of a King

© 2022 by Sal Cerra. All rights reserved.
Destiny Fire Ministries

No part of this book may be reproduced without written permission from the publisher or copyright holder, nor may any part of this book be transmitted in any form or by any means electronic, mechanical, photocopying, recording, or other, without prior written permission from the publisher or copyright holder.

Unless otherwise noted, all scripture quotations are from the New King James Version®. Copyright © 1982 by Thomas Nelson. Used by permission. All rights reserved.

Scripture quotations marked (NLT) are taken from the *Holy Bible,* New Living Translation, copyright © ©1996, 2004, 2007, 2013, 2015 by Tyndale House Foundation. Used by permission of Tyndale House Publishers Inc., Carol Stream, Illinois 60188. All rights reserved.

Scripture quotations marked (NIV) are taken from the Holy Bible, NEW INTERNATIONAL VERSION®, NIV® Copyright © 1973, 1978, 1984, 2011 by Biblica, Inc.® Used by permission. All rights reserved worldwide.

Scripture quotations are from the ESV® Bible (The Holy Bible, English Standard Version®), copyright © 2001 by Crossway, a publishing ministry of Good News Publishers. Used by permission. All rights reserved.

Scripture quotations marked TPT are from The Passion Translation®. Copyright © 2017, 2018, 2020 by Passion & Fire Ministries, Inc. Used by permission. All rights reserved. ThePassionTranslation.com.

ISBN: 978-1-7349742-2-5 (Print)

       978-1-7349742-3-2 (Digital)

Printed in the United States of America

What a beautiful treasure the Lord has blessed me with in my wonderful wife, Kristine. I can't imagine walking into destiny without you. You are a special lifeline who has learned how to deal with my prophetic craziness. There's no possible way this book could have come to life without your insight and input. I want everyone reading this to know that you were the one who wrote the beautiful allegories portraying our King Jesus coming back for His spotless bride. You were able to see my vision and bring it to life in these fun, creative stories throughout the pages of this book. You have the ability to take my stones and help me turn them into diamonds. I truly love you like crazy and am so looking forward to spending the rest of my life here with you, as well as the ages to come. You're beautiful and radiant, and you speak life into me, sometimes without even realizing it. You are my perfect destiny partner to come alongside my King Jesus. Thank you!

With love,

Sal

Contents

Foreword	11
Introduction	13
Part 1: Seeing Your True Reflection	**17**
Chapter 1: The Mirror	19
Chapter 2: Destiny Sees	29
Part 2: Premature Royalty	**39**
Chapter 3: Disorderly Conduct	41
Chapter 4: Childish Delights	53
Chapter 5: Unfinished Business	69
Part 3: Life of the King	**89**
Chapter 6: Supreme Royalty	93
Chapter 7: Kingdom Inheritance	109
Chapter 8: Supreme Influence	125
Part 4: The Bridal Company	**137**
Chapter 9: The Desperate Cry	141
Chapter 10: Finding First Love	151
Chapter 11: Snow White	163
Part 5: Destiny Mirrors	**173**
Chapter 12: Waves of Glory	177
Chapter 13: Glorious Reflections	191
Chapter 14: Here Comes the Bride	205

Foreword

Over ten years ago, a young man contacted me who went to the church we attended. At that time in his life, God was using him in ministry with an emphasis on functioning in the gifts, but he was not satisfied. We began a relationship that has lasted and strengthened over the years. I have watched him grow in his relationship with the Lord to the place where he could hear God say, "Write the vision and make it plain."

I have witnessed him grow in many of the revelations he shares in this book. The seeds of these truths are working in his life. When he speaks of preparation and the deep inner-dealings of God, I know that he has genuine knowledge of these things because I have walked with him through a number of them.

One day I asked the Lord what the glory of God was that we are to behold "in the glass" or mirror in 2 Corinthians 3:18. He said, "The glory of God is what I have done in you." I have watched God work this glory in Sal. When he beholds that in the mirror, it gives him incentive to let God dig deeper and remove all that inhibits his relationship with the heavenly bridegroom.

As Sal lays out the preparation of the bridal company for our King, it is accented by his own encounters and visitations with the Lord. His understanding of applying the principles he shares will give the reader pause for reflection and meditation.

I encourage the reader to use this book in two ways:

1. As an inspiration, allowing God to stir up a hunger in you for the King.
2. As a devotional, praying into those truths that witness to their spirit.

I highly recommend *The King's Bridal Company* to those who desire to grow in God.

Lord increase the hunger of all who read to grow up into Him in all things!

—Dr. Wm. J. Hurst

President, The Institute for Strategic Christian Leadership

Introduction

I never imagined in my lifetime I would see or experience some of the things that are happening in our world today. We are living in eye-opening times. To some of us, it looks like all hope is lost. Fear has gripped this world, and many people are living day-to-day wondering if it will all come crashing down or suddenly come to an end. I know one thing is for sure—this crazy world has really gotten people thinking about one thing—the return of Jesus. At least it has for me.

What do these days look like in the eyes of the church, and what is the church supposed to represent in the eyes of the world? I believe we are living in the end times. So what is the end-time church supposed to look like? Scripture tells us that Jesus is returning for a pure, spotless people.

> **In these last days, Jesus is looking for a company of intimate lovers, ones who want to spend every waking minute in His presence.**

In these last days, Jesus is looking for a company of intimate lovers, ones who want to spend every waking minute in His presence. These are people who want to reflect who He truly is. More than anything, they want to represent a mirror image of the heart of the Father.

These people I'm talking about are ones who want to come to the end of themselves—to become so desperate for Him that they know nothing else. They are sold-out lovers to the King. These lovers want to be conformed into the image of His Son, Jesus. They want to represent His character and nature. Others will be drawn to these special people because of the atmosphere they carry—His presence. This special group of people I am talking about is called the Bridal Company.

Throughout my life, the Lord has given me numerous supernatural encounters. You will find many throughout the pages of this book. There is one in particular that I want to share with you now. I believe when the Lord gave me this encounter, He was showing me a glorious reflection of what was to come.

I was spending some time with the Lord when I was caught up by the Holy Spirit and suddenly lifted above the earth into the heavenlies—it was absolutely breathtaking! As I was taking in my surroundings, I looked down, and to my surprise, I saw a majestic golden city. I knew instantly that this was not an earthly city. Every part of the city was made of pure gold. The glow that emanated from the city drew me closer. I was mesmerized by the appearance of this golden city and how pristine it was! The dimensions were exact—every wall was perfectly matched in height. The city was so striking that I knew it could have only come from heaven. During this particular encounter, the Lord only allowed me a glimpse of this marvelous city. Just as I was coming closer to the city, the Lord brought me back to my natural realm.

A few months later when I was seeking His face, I was taken back to the golden city. Nothing had changed—it was exactly as I remembered it. I wanted to take in as much as I possibly could, and I didn't want it to stop! When my incredible encounter ended, I asked the Lord why He was showing me this beautiful, golden city. He told me that this was the city He was preparing for His Bridal Company.

Introduction

> Then I, John, saw the holy city, New Jerusalem, coming down out of heaven from God, prepared as a bride adorned for her husband. (Revelation 21:2)

This book was birthed out of what the Lord placed on my heart. As He downloaded the pages in this book, I began to see it in "parts." Each section leads back to one central message—preparing the Bridal Company for His return. At the beginning of each section, you will also read a fairytale about a lost kingdom that slowly unravels a love story. The story continues through each part of the book and introduces the reader to the theme of each section. This story comes alive as the king prepares his only son to redeem the paradise they once had. Come along inside this book and read as the prince, heir to the throne, returns from the battle of a lifetime and becomes the king he was destined for. And what is a love story without a wedding? Will the new king find his one-and-only true love and make her his bride?

I feel led by the Holy Spirit to bring an awareness of what the Bridal Company should represent in these last days and what the Father's heart is for His people. His heart's desire is for us to be transformed into the image of His son, Jesus Christ, and to live life the way He intended as true sons and daughters of King Jesus—and as heirs to His throne.

I pray that this book will bless your spirit and prepare your heart as we get closer to the return of our King. May the pages within this book awaken your spirit, soul, and body as you learn how to demonstrate a glorious, mirrored reflection of the Father's Son, Jesus Christ. He's coming back for His spotless bride. Are you ready?

Part 1: Seeing Your True Reflection

Through our hurts and pain, God can reveal things that are hindering or blocking our growth in Him. In this first section, we will dive deep into looking within ourselves. I will share my own journey of how the Lord lovingly showed me my weaknesses and hindrances holding me captive from moving forward into the destiny He planned for my life. I pray that my own continued process of transformation will help you as you walk out your own journey of knowing your true identity and who your real Daddy is. Everything has a beginning…..who are you really? What does your true reflection say about you?

The Lost Kingdom

The day had finally arrived when his son was born into the world. He was beautiful and perfect in his father's eyes. Overwhelming love filled the king's heart. The boy's parents had been waiting many years to conceive a child. Not just any child, but a son who would inherit the kingdom. He would be king someday. And not just any king. A king above all kings. A king who would bring righteousness and restore the kingdom back to its original intent. He would redeem all that was lost.

At one time, the kingdom had been a beautiful paradise. Everything that lived in the kingdom flourished and thrived. Everyone was happy, and goodness flowed from their hearts. Over the years, the king started to see his kingdom deteriorate. An enemy had slowly started to infiltrate his people. Some of the people who were once righteous were now contaminated with evil in their hearts. They had turned away from their king and his ways. His kingdom had become divided between good and evil. He wanted to save his people from further destruction and despair. The king's heart desired to bring back his kingdom to the fullness it was created for.

The king held his new son in his arms. As the king looked down into the little prince's eyes, he saw his reflection. He saw a king staring back at him. He cried tears of joy as he knew in that moment that his sweet, innocent son was sent to be the savior of the kingdom. The king understood what he had to do. His son would have to make the ultimate sacrifice. He was their only hope.

Chapter 1: The Mirror

Have you ever heard the phrase, *the mirror never lies*? It's amazing that a shiny surface is able to reflect the truth back to us—whether we want to see it or not!

We know that everything in the physical world is a representation of the spiritual realm. And it's interesting to note that the way light is reflected in the natural has a great correlation to how the light of the Lord is reflected through our own lives.

When speaking about science, there is a term called "transmission of light," which, in its most simple definition, is the determination of how much light can pass through one item and into the next. As Christians, our goal in this life is for the light of Jesus to pass on to others through us so that they can also be changed and transformed, just like we have been.

There is another phenomenon that takes place in the natural called absorption, which happens when light is collected (or absorbed) by an object instead of reflecting it. When light is absorbed, the process of transmission is stopped or reduced. Likewise, when there are things in our lives that stop the light of Christ from shining through us, we can't fully reflect Him to those around us. How much of His reflection is being warped or distorted to the world because of the way we choose to live?

In order for us to really reflect Jesus in our lives, we have to first take a long look in the mirror and come face-to-face with our true reflection.

Only when we really see the things that need to be changed can we take action and see a transformation.

Hidden Identities

Most of us at one point in our lives have experienced the "hidden-identity syndrome," as I like to call it. You meet someone and hit it off right away, and before you know it, you are developing a friendship with this person. In the beginning, your relationship is going great—you're texting, talking, hanging out. Life is good. But after a while, you realize that the friend you once thought you knew isn't really that person at all. This individual was masking something while they were getting to know you. Their true character and nature begin to surface, and somewhere underneath it all, you wonder where your friend went. We've all had that person in our lives at one time or another. From childhood through our adult years, friends come and go; it's a fact of life.

We all have stuff. Let's face it; no one is perfect. I like to think that all of us are unique. Well, in reality, we are. God created each of us to have our own spirit, soul, and body with a purpose and special gifts. The world would be pretty boring if we were all created the same. I can't imagine a world full of Sals! There are things other people have and can do that I don't have or can't do. It truly is amazing when we think about the creation of human beings. God loves us so much that He created us in His own image. Have you really thought about that? We were created in the likeness of God the Father. That blows me away! So why is it that I am not perfect?

At one time in my life, I was an arrogant, prideful, know-it-all who felt he was entitled. Yes, sad to say it, that was me. No one could tell me anything because I knew it all. I was flying high with all the answers. Lucky for me, God got a hold of me. The day I gave my life to the Lord, I changed dramatically. My spiritual eyes were open to a whole new world. I could see things in me that suddenly began to change for the better. Yet, there was still something missing. There were parts of me that still needed work. I look back now and can see how much the Lord

Chapter 1: The Mirror

has changed my life over the years. Who I really was in God's eyes was not the person I was portraying on the outside—even after I came to know Him.

> **God loves us so much that He created us in His own image.**

We may even think that we have the answer for everything because we're born again. Unfortunately, because we don't know what we are supposed to look like to the world; we often don't represent Jesus as the awesome, loving King that He is.

> But grow in the grace and knowledge of our Lord and Savior Jesus Christ. To Him *be* the glory both now and forever. Amen. (2 Peter 3:18)

At the moment of salvation, we come to the understanding that our sins have been forgiven, but we frequently have a misconception that our lifestyle and character will also be transformed.

Many of us are walking around with hidden identities. We don't know who we truly are in Jesus Christ—our true identity. We live day-to-day without even realizing that who God made us to be is not who we truly are. Even the best of us do not like who we are sometimes. We want to change but don't have a clue what to do. Believe it or not, the answer lies within us.

Transformation Is a Process

Sadly, we repeatedly find that the nature we exemplify is a nature that is contrary to our king. I am the first to admit that I was the person who understood that Jesus wiped away my sins and made me new when I became a Christian. However, I assumed that the "new me" was instantly fixed in every way. Boy, did I get a wake-up call! Don't get me wrong—my life did change for the better when I accepted Christ, but I (the old nature trying to rise up again) got in the way. We become born again; yet remain in a completely fallen and corrupt world. Temptation still lurks around each corner. This is why Paul wrote the verses below.

> But you have not so learned Christ, if indeed you have heard Him and have been taught by Him, as the truth is in Jesus: that you put off, concerning your former conduct, the old man which grows corrupt according to the deceitful lusts, and be renewed in the spirit of your mind, and that you put on the new man which was created according to God, in true righteousness and holiness. (Ephesians 4:20-24).

The Apostle Paul is reminding us here that in order to take on the nature of Christ, we need to put off our former ways of conducting ourselves. We need to allow the Holy Spirit to renew our minds so we can live in true righteousness and holiness the way God intended.

When I was born again, I was on a spiritual high, and that led me to believe that I had all the answers. As I progressed through my spiritual journey, the Lord, in His mercy, always had His hand on me. He waited and waited while I went around the mountain of life many times over and showered me with patience and love.

The Broken Mirror

As my shallow spiritual high began to descend, my true spiritual nature (my heavenly eyes) started to open. This is when I started to take a good look at myself in the mirror. The eyes of my heart began to see the man in the mirror. I looked in the mirror every day and saw what looked like me. My reflection stared back at me—and I didn't like what I was seeing.

> For if anyone is a hearer of the word and not a doer, he is like a man observing his natural face in a mirror; (James 1:23)

Chapter 1: The Mirror

It wasn't the outside reflection that bothered me the most; it was the inner-refraction, a bent form of His glorious image trying to work in and through me, which I couldn't comprehend. What was the problem here? It definitely wasn't Christ, because nothing about Him is bent in any way. The problem was resting deep within me.

How could there be a problem? In my early years of salvation, I did everything I could to learn and grow in Him. I went to church, studied my Bible, worshiped, and sought Him every moment I could. I hopped from conference to conference seeking a spiritual high, and traveled overseas to do missionary work. I was doing and grasping everything that I could to walk out my Christian life. It's what I thought God wanted me to do. I was at a point in my life where I should have been happy, but I wasn't. I was going through a very difficult time, and I didn't know what to do other than seek the Lord.

The Mirror's Image

In this desperate time, I cried out to Him for answers. I was deep in prayer one day, and the next thing I knew, I was in a trance. What I saw shook me to the core. During this experience, I was staring at a mirror. As I was looking at myself, I suddenly saw half of my face start to blacken with decay and melt away. It seemed so life-like that I thought I was playing out a scene in a horror movie! I couldn't watch anymore as my face deteriorated, so I turned my head away. I took a deep breath to get a hold of myself. What just happened? I wanted to make sure what I saw was really what I was seeing with my own eyes, so I turned my head back toward the mirror.

At first, I thought, "Oh, thank goodness! It was just my imagination." I stared at my reflection in the mirror, and looking back at me was my normal face. But then it happened again! Once again, my face started turning black and melting away. I felt like I was in a nightmare, not an experience with the Lord. What was happening? Still in the encounter, I ran out of the house with my tormented self and asked the Lord what was going on. At that exact moment, I was back in my room where it all started.

This experience caused such a stir in me that I couldn't stop thinking about it. For the next few weeks, the image of my face decaying in the mirror consumed my thoughts. I had to know why the Lord showed me what He did. So I asked Him again, "What happened in that experience, Lord? Why did You show me that?" I didn't get an answer right away, but I kept asking and seeking one. Every time I looked at myself in the mirror, I thought about that encounter. Why was my heart unsettled every time I looked at my reflection?

Day in and day out I would ask the Lord. I waited and waited. Finally, He answered with a question for me. I heard Him ask, "Do you really want the truth?" As hard as it was hearing God speak the truth about me, I wanted to know. He said, "Every time you look in the mirror, you are not looking at a true representation of who I really am. When people look at you, they don't see Me."

> He said, "Every time you look in the mirror, you are not looking at a true representation of who I really am. When people look at you, they don't see Me."

Ouch! That truth hit hard, and there went the "me" I thought I was striving to be! In one statement, the Lord deflated my pride, selfish plans, and everything about me that I thought I was, but really wasn't at all. I started to look beyond the man in the mirror and wanted to get to the heart of the matter. What were people really seeing when they looked at me?

This process brought a lot of mixed thoughts and feelings. Emotions flooded through me often. I felt disgusted with myself. Slowly, God started to reveal hidden truths about me—raw hard facts of who I was pretending to be and exactly who I needed to become.

Chapter 1: The Mirror

Sometimes the truth hurts. But God isn't trying to intentionally hurt us; He wants to perfect us into His image. As His unconditional love continued to pour over me, I started to discover who I really was through His eyes. This is where my transformation of the "new me" began.

Hitting Rock Bottom

When I discovered the truth of who I was in my own eyes, I hit rock bottom. I felt that I let God down. But He, being such a good Father, remained steadfast on who I was to become and not focused on how I lived in my past.

The Lord showed me different areas about my life that He needed to reveal in order to heal me deep inside. That's what He does—He brings out memories, feelings, traumas, convictions, and whatever it takes to reconcile the wounds caused throughout our lifetime.

> He heals the brokenhearted and binds up their wounds.
> (Psalm 147:3)

These wounds keep us captive to Satan's patterns still mixed in our lives, and in order to mask the pain and maintain our self-soothing defenses, we make excuses, build walls, and develop coping mechanisms to "get through life." God loves us so much that He doesn't want us walking through life with destructive patterns and negative behaviors. God wants to redeem, restore, and transform us so nothing can hold us back from walking into the destiny that He has been dreaming for our lives.

Isn't that exciting? God wants to make us whole again so we can have the full experience of His love for us. God wants to set us completely free. To be honest, when I first got saved, I didn't realize what it truly meant to be set free the way I understand it now. Most of us don't even know we need to be set free. We can be so caught up with our normal routines and days of living life in the world that we sometimes don't realize what's really happening inside of us. And what pastor or preacher is actually talking about this kind of stuff at church? Normally, we hear the exact opposite, which is: "Christ just came into your life, and now all of your outside and inner problems are gone for good." This is far from the truth!

Many of us don't want to go through the process of revealing the pain that God wants to bring to the surface so He can heal us. When God started working in my life, I felt like an onion, with each layer being peeled back piece by piece. The inner-wounds that I needed to be set free from were areas I buried from my childhood or other parts of my past. God doesn't want us to cover them up. He wants to unravel them for us, but He won't go against our free will. One of the reasons He wants us set free is because the enemy uses these past wounds, traumas, and areas of captivity to keep us spiritually bound and away from walking in our destiny.

Being Set Free

There are many beliefs about healing and deliverance, and I won't go into depth about them in this book. Some people believe that you are healed and delivered all at once or that it was taken care of at the cross. It's like a "one-and-done" concept. I don't believe that—that's just my opinion. I say this because I have walked through it and I'm still walking through it. Sanctification and transformation is a life-long journey and is a part of the process of being conformed into the image of His Son, Jesus Christ.

There was a time in my life when I went through intense healing and deliverance and I had the most incredible experience. I was in my hotel reading Ephesians 3 and fell into a trance. All of a sudden, the walls and ceiling started shaking. I came out of the trance stunned. I closed my eyes for about thirty seconds and re-opened them. The walls and ceiling were still shaking. I thought I was in the middle of an earthquake. I immediately called my friend Tim and asked him if there was an earthquake in the city. He started to laugh and probably thought I was a little crazy, but he was totally cool about it. We hung up, and I sat there wondering if I was losing my mind. As I sat on the bed, I heard the Lord speak to me. He said, "Everything is beginning to shake off of you. I am shaking you out of your inner prison." I was completely blown away by

Chapter 1: The Mirror

what I just heard. This encounter drove me deeper into my healing and deliverance. I knew I was being set free.

The Lord doesn't want us walking through life broken and hurting. He wants to take all the ugly pieces of our life and make them beautiful. If God were to heal and deliver us from everything all at once, how could we learn to overcome the roadblocks that prevent us from walking into the fullness of our destiny?

> **True destiny looks like Jesus Christ. So if you truly want to look and act like Jesus, then this is where your process begins—with yourself.**

True destiny looks like Jesus Christ. So if you truly want to look and act like Jesus, then this is where your process begins—with yourself. You have to *want* to go through the process. Jesus died on the cross so we could walk out an abundance of life with the Father. Why do we sometimes feel that we are not living the life God intended for us after salvation? Why do we stumble over roadblocks or feel trapped at times? This is where we need answers. We need truth, and the only One who can help us is our Father. But the Father won't help us if we don't ask for His help. He won't just give us the answers.

> *It is* the glory of God to conceal a matter, but the glory of kings *is* to search out a matter. (Proverbs 25:2)

God wants us to search things out ourselves because there is something we must learn along the way through the process. And usually, the thing that is blocking the way is ourselves. We must learn to come to the end of ourselves and get out of our own way to be totally set free.

The King's Bridal Company

> Then He said to *them* all, "If anyone desires to come after Me, let him deny himself, and take up his cross daily, and follow Me." (Luke 9:23)

We have to desire and chase after Him. In order to truly follow Christ, you have to be willing to get out of the way (deny yourself) so you can be transformed into His character and nature (following Him and His heart). In the garden of Gethsemane, even Jesus had to lay down His will and follow the will of His Father (Mark 14:36). As followers of Jesus Christ, we also have to learn to surrender our will to the Father. After all, Jesus is the Pattern Son.

Chapter 2: Destiny Sees

The New Me

As I was going through my healing and deliverance, I began to look at myself in the mirror with new eyes. I started to like the new man in the mirror that was looking back at me. I believed that I was doing everything to represent the character and nature of Jesus. In everything I did or said, I would ask myself, "What would Jesus do?" This helped me with emotions and reactions in my interactions with people. I became a better person to be around. My family and friends started to take notice and wondered what happened to me. I had a complete character overhaul. Things that used to offend or bother me didn't anymore. I developed a great empathy toward others. I also had a better understanding of where people were at because I was once there. I began to see those around me through Jesus' eyes. I wanted to become a better husband, father, son, brother, and friend.

You may think this sounds easy to transform into a new you. But I will tell you that God brings things out of you that you may not want to face. It may be difficult and painful and you may go through intense spiritual battles. Like I mentioned before, God wants to peel back the layers to get to the root of the problems in your life. He loves you so much that He wants to heal the wounds that were buried for so long. You may have experienced trauma as a child, and you have hidden the memories so deep that sometimes it feels like it never happened. You may have iniquity in your bloodline that you knew nothing about and can't understand why you can never get ahead financially, or you are constantly worried about money. Sickness, disease, and curses also carry through our bloodlines. These are things God wants to expose so you can be set free.

The enemy places blockages in your life that will prevent you from walking into the fullness of what God has for you. He wants to redeem and restore you to what He originally made you to be. Please understand that God never intended for us to walk around this world brokenhearted and filled with pain. He wants to purify and refine you into gold because that is how He sees you. Though the process may be painful at times, He will always be by your side. He will never leave you or give up on you.

> And the Lord, He is the One who goes before you. He
> will be with you, He will not leave you nor forsake you;
> do not fear nor be dismayed. (Deuteronomy 31:8)

Are you ready to be turned into something amazing? Are you ready to be the best person you can be? I want you to know this: you have to WANT it! You have to want to change for the better. Not for yourself, but because you want to represent the One who lives inside of you, to be able to draw people in because there is something so special about you that everyone wants some of what you have. You have to choose to leave your old ways behind.

> Do not remember the former things, nor consider the
> things of old. (Isaiah 43:18)

Remember, we all have free will. God doesn't force us into anything. You have to WANT to be like Him. You were created for that purpose. God created us in the likeness of Him. When you make the decision to change your life for the better, God will see you through.

As you progress through the healing process, you will see clearer and it will become easier as God works in you. As you feel better, your

Chapter 2: Destiny Sees

willingness for healing and deliverance will increase as your wounds are healed and a new you takes over. Many people are under oppression and will physically feel the weight lift off of them. You will feel a spring in your step as the new you begins to transform.

So, you've made the decision to let God do His work in you. Notice I said, "let God." You have to give the Lord permission to work in your life. Psalm 51:10 says, "Create in me a clean heart, O God, and renew a steadfast spirit within me." He will not violate someone's free will, but He will constantly remind you that He wants to heal you, redeem you, and restore you. Listen to His still, small voice. He's waiting for you to say, "Yes, Lord! Let Your will be done in me."

How long will it take? How will it happen? What will it look like? Everyone is different because we all have diverse life stories. Let me fill you in on a little secret: it isn't a one-size-fits-all method or a one-and-done. Healing and deliverance is a lifetime commitment. It takes patience and a love affair with our heavenly Father. For myself, I receive "maintenance" checkups as I need them. I went through about four years of intense healing and deliverance with a counselor. Now when God shows me something I need to work on, I speak with my counselor, and not just any counselor—she is specialized in healing and deliverance. She has a gift for ushering in the presence of God so I can look deep within myself.

My personal relationships are so much better because of the process I have been through with healing and deliverance. My marriage, my relationship with my children, my parents, my siblings, and my friends are all a work in progress. I know I am being the best person I can be because I am allowing God to work in my life. When we allow God to work in our lives, we start to have a new perspective on how we look at ourselves and how God sees us. We need to understand how important it is for our vision to line up with our Father's vision.

Who's Your Daddy?

What would it be like growing up in a kingdom with the king as our daddy? We could look at it in two ways. We could accept who we are as the king's heir, or we could be rebellious and go against everything intended for us as true royal heirs. We have a choice as true sons and daughters of our heavenly Father. We have free will to choose to follow in His footsteps, or we can choose to follow what is not of Him.

When we choose not to follow Him, we are choosing to live in the world system rather than in His kingdom. When we decide to do things on our own, we abandon the Father's will. The good news is that we can't hide from Him no matter what we choose. He loves us so much that He will follow us to the ends of the earth. He will do everything in His power to seek us out. We sometimes may think to ourselves, "Where are you, God?" or "Here I am! Come find me!" Even though He may seem distant at times, He is always there, watching our every move, loving us every step of the way.

> **When we get to the place where we want nothing but Jesus, then He will come to us and begin to make us whole again.**

Sometimes God wants us to wait on Him so we become desperate for Him. When we get to the place where we want nothing but Jesus, then He will come to us and begin to make us whole again. That's how I felt when I began to look at myself in the mirror again.

Wow! Looking Good, Man

As I was looking in the mirror, I started to see a different man staring back at me. I began to have a different perspective on who God really was in my life. My mindset started to shift toward seeing God as a Father and me as His son. During the time of my healing and deliverance when I allowed God to work in my life, I came to realize that God is an all-loving Father, regardless of my shortcomings. He knows all of our hang-

Chapter 2: Destiny Sees

ups in life. He sees the trauma, vows, judgments, soul ties—everything that holds us back from truly knowing our Daddy and His love for us.

One of the first revelations that God brought to the surface was my relationship with my earthly father. He showed me that my view of my father was distorted. Even though my relationship with my father seemed okay on the outside, there were many deep hurts and wounds from my relationship with him as I was growing up. Because I couldn't see beyond my father's own inner pain and shortcomings, I was unable to see my father the way the Lord intended for me to see him. Many of us have a hard time accepting who God really is to us, a loving Father, full of mercy and goodness.

> Oh, give thanks to the Lord, for *He is* good! For His mercy *endures* forever. (1 Chronicles 16:34)

We feel this way because of the broken relationships we have with our earthly fathers. It's Father God's desire for us to have all of our relationships restored. When His desire becomes our desire, we start to see through His lens. It is through this heavenly lens that we start to think about how God sees us and how we see ourselves. Wow, God is so good!

Does He Really See Me Like That?

As I was beginning to have this new perspective on how God sees me, I was astonished to learn just how much I did not know my Father in heaven. This new point of view was causing me to have a paradigm shift, and I realized at that moment that I had the most amazing Father.

I began to see that Father God wasn't this ruler who governed the universe with a gavel. I used to think that He was judging me and would say, "You've done this!" or "You've done that!" or "Sal, you've messed up again!" Of course, there were many times I messed up—and believe me, I have messed up big time! But God is so amazing! He showed me that He's not in the business of condemnation. It says in Romans 8:1, "There is therefore now no condemnation to those who are in Christ

Jesus, who do not walk according to the flesh, but according to the Spirit." God wasn't against me; God was for me.

I started to see Him as my biggest cheerleader. God is rooting for us. He allows us to see the hurts and hang-ups so we can overcome them. God knows we're going to make mistakes, and in the process, He is hoping we will seek Him and want His guidance. I believe God allows us to see our sin to help us overcome it and grow in our relationship with Him.

It's a Mystery

So how does God really see us? There are so many places throughout the Bible that tell us how God sees us. Before we go there, I want to give you an insight into God's revelation to Paul on the mystery of Christ. Ephesians 3:3-4 says, "How that by revelation He made known to me the mystery (as I have briefly written already, you may understand my knowledge in the mystery of Christ),"

Why do we need to know the mystery before we can understand how God sees us? It is important for us to understand what the mystery really is. This mystery has been hidden since the beginning of the ages.

> And to make all see what *is* the fellowship of the mystery, which from the beginning of the ages has been hidden in God who created all things through Jesus Christ. (Ephesians 3:9)

Colossians 1:26-27 says this:

> The mystery which has been hidden from ages and from generations, but now has been revealed to His saints. To them God willed to make known what are the riches of the glory of this mystery among the Gentiles: which is Christ in you, the hope of glory.

Chapter 2: Destiny Sees

When I finally understood that God lives within me and He is the hope of glory, I said, "Wow, God chose us before the beginning of the ages to host His glorious presence within us!" Let's think about that. Before he laid the foundations of the earth, He had a master plan that included us. This should tell you how valuable you are to the King. When He sees you, He's looking at a reflection of His Son, Jesus Christ. After all, He's the one who said that the mystery of Christ lives within us, so when He sees us, He sees us as carriers of His glory.

When God sees you, He sees right through your faults, your weaknesses, and your mistakes. I believe that when He looks at us, He sees us as the greatness He created us to be. He is so fascinated with us. He longs for us to seek Him because He can't wait to reveal Himself to us. He is just waiting for us to catch a glimpse of His love, so we will chase after Him and seek His face.

> When He looks at us, He sees us as the greatness He created us to be.

Imagine yourself as a young child running through the fields, and you become fascinated with a beautiful butterfly and begin to chase it. Your focus is to catch the butterfly. In the process, you might stumble and fall a few times, but you finally reach the butterfly and catch it!

Think about that butterfly. How can God create something so delicate and full of life? This beautiful creature was once an ugly caterpillar, transformed into a beautiful butterfly. A butterfly's life cycle is so incredible if you think about it. The butterfly begins as an egg and then becomes a caterpillar. From a caterpillar, it weaves itself into a chrysalis and waits while it is transformed into a butterfly. It takes time for this beautiful creature to come forth. When the butterfly is ready to emerge, the chrysalis breaks open. But the butterfly isn't quite ready to take off just yet. It has to wait for the wings to dry. There is also a liquid called hemolymph that is pumped into the wings to make them big and strong.

You may think you are an ugly caterpillar with nothing to offer, but God sees you for the beauty you were created for. He gives you purpose so you can fly! You may stumble and fall a few times in the process, but He's right there to pick you back up. When you're ready to take off and fly, He's pumping you up, drying off your wings, and giving you the strength you need to go on. That's how God sees you.

It's His hope and desire that when we chase after Him, we will be willing to go through the transformation process to become what He has called us to be—His greatest masterpiece. God created each and every one of us in His image. When we look into the mirror, He wants us to see beyond the glass—to look inside of ourselves and see the hope of glory that He forged within us before the foundations of the earth. God sees you as one of His greatest creations of all time. He uniquely designed you, intricately wove you together, and loved you to life.

Heavenly Perspective

Being able to recognize how God truly sees you affects our understanding of how we see ourselves. Knowing that we are the apple of God's eye and that when He sees us, He sees greatness and not failure, helps us have confidence. First Peter 2:9 tells us, "But you are a chosen generation, a royal priesthood, a holy nation, His own special people, that you may proclaim the praises of Him who called you out of darkness into His marvelous light;" Wow! He chooses us, calls us royalty, and we are considered to be His own special people! He calls us out of our depths of despair and brings us into His glorious light of freedom and life! He sees us as righteous, not wicked; beautiful, not ugly; courageous, not timid. Understanding how God sees us influences how we see ourselves. If God is for us, why would we be against ourselves? If God sees beauty, then we are not ugly. If He sees greatness, then we are not failures.

Looking in the mirror and seeing greatness is a little different than seeing failure, and it will affect the way that you view others. When you see people's failures with eyes of greatness, those failures won't be the focus of your outlook on them. The failures will become part

Chapter 2: Destiny Sees

of the solution in helping them walk into that greatness. When you see those who are disrespectful and rude through the eyes of greatness, you will see the pain and suffering they have endured and become more empathetic toward their behavior.

> **If we can't see from a heavenly perspective, how can we manifest the kingdom to others?**

The way we see ourselves can be so crucial towards helping others walk into their destiny. Seeing ourselves with the eyes of God will begin to thrust others on a pathway to greatness. We are designed to walk in the character and nature of Christ to bring greatness into a dying world. If we can't see from a heavenly perspective, how can we manifest the kingdom to others?

Part 2: Premature Royalty

Whether we are new believers or we've been walking with the Lord most of our lives, the Lord wants us to continually grow and learn His ways. As we allow Him to transform and mold us, we should want to learn to stay firmly grounded. There is always something new the Holy Spirit is teaching or showing us, and we should get so excited that we will want to run with it. This section focuses on some areas of our lives where we can get carried away without even realizing it. I don't want to miss what God has for me, and I'm pretty sure if you are reading this book, you don't want to miss it either!

Come Find Me

"Ready or not, here I come!" says the king. He turns around and sees his little prince standing in the middle of the room with his eyes covered. The boy thinks because he can't "see" his father, that his father can't see him either.

The king smiles and begins to "look" for the boy. The anxious little prince can't stand it anymore and pulls his hands away and yells, "Here I am!"

The King's Bridal Company

The king grabs his son and twirls him into the air, the boy squealing with excitement. The prince doesn't have a care in the world. He trusts his father with all his heart as he flies through the air in his father's arms. They have a bond that only a father and son can share.

As the king gently sets his son down, the little prince looks up into his father's eyes and says, "I want to be just like you, Father, when I grow up!"

The king looks down and as if looking in a mirror, seeing himself in his son. He stands before the carefree child, thinking about the vast kingdom that he will one day inherit. He watches as the young prince laughs and runs away to find a new adventure. The little boy is full of innocence and curiosity.

The king hopes that through the years of joys and sorrows to come that he will always remember his love for his father. He also knows there will be trials that the prince will one day have to endure.

A cry breaks through the king's thoughts. His little prince has fallen and skinned his knee. The king goes running to his son and picks him up immediately to give comfort. The boy nestles into his father's arms and calms down. As the king gently rocks his son back and forth, the boy peacefully drifts off to sleep.

The two snuggle together for a long while. The king knows that this is just one of many little bumps and bruises his son will get in life, and he will love him through each and every one. He smiles to himself as he looks forward to watching his son mature into the fullness he was destined for.

Chapter 3: Disorderly Conduct

When we are born into this world, we arrive kicking and screaming as tiny, helpless babes. With the help of those around us, we learn how to function physically, emotionally, and socially. Our parents, grandparents, aunts, and uncles—or anyone close to us—guide us toward learning how to walk, talk, and eat. They also show us how to receive and give love. As we grow and mature, we need the support of others to show us how to express ourselves and develop meaningful relationships.

It is very important for a baby to be held and loved in order to develop properly. Babies need to be nurtured, loved, and cared for to ensure that they will reach their full potential in life. They depend on the people closest to them to help them develop the skills needed to lead healthy, successful lives. Children who are isolated or ignored do not develop as they should compared to children who are in intimate relationships.

Children are born with the instinct to survive. They are full of curiosity and are eager to learn new things. But curiosity can sometimes lead them into trouble. Think about a new baby who has just learned to crawl and pull themselves up. Your first reaction is to "baby-proof" your home to keep them safe. We also have to teach them to stay out of trouble and learn to discipline with a firm, but loving hand.

As new believers, we are born again as babies. Just as our parents taught us how to walk, talk, and eat, the Lord wants to teach us to walk, talk, and eat in the Spirit.

> Train up a child in the way he should go, and when he is old he will not depart from it. (Proverbs 22:6)

When we learned to walk, many of us didn't just stand up and take off running. We had to learn to take "baby steps" and learn to gain confidence and strength to be able to walk steadily. You had to learn how to put one foot in front of the other. That's how it is when you learn to walk in the Spirit. Many of us want to "take off" running full-speed. If we do, we may miss something important along the way that the Lord wants to show us. We want to be "led" by His Spirit, not by ours or anyone else's. As with anything we try to do in life, things tend to get in the way of our progress.

Unhealthy Mindsets

Many of us are born into a religion or have knowledge of a religion. For me, I remember going to church my entire childhood. Religion was composed of rituals and repetition that kept me away from knowing who God truly was and what He represented. My relationship was with the leader of the church. I found myself seeking the head of the church rather than seeking out the Lord. What I really knew was the ways of the church and traditions. I didn't know the ways of an intimate Father.

Every denomination has some sort of customary beliefs or practices. They have their own patterns, behaviors, or mindsets. Religious values can create unhealthy mindsets. I was so wrapped up in "the ways," that these mindsets became an idol to me. My focus was on being concerned if I was saying or doing the right thing. As a result, I became incapable of knowing who God really was. I learned about God and the ways of the church rather than knowing Him personally.

Remember when I said that children who are isolated or ignored can't fully develop compared to children who have intimate relationships? It

CHAPTER 3: DISORDERLY CONDUCT

is the same with our heavenly Father. We need to have a healthy, intimate relationship with Him to fully develop into what He has planned for us. I was chasing a religion (traditions and ways of the church) rather than chasing the King himself and His ways for my life.

> **I was chasing a religion (traditions and ways of the church) rather than chasing the King himself and His ways for my life.**

Powerless Pursuit

Life without meaning is powerless. I was in pursuit of something that had no meaning and no power. What do I mean by that? For starters, I didn't own a Bible or read one. Yes, that's right—I was in pursuit of something that had no meaning, so in return, I became powerless. I went to church and would rely on man-made ways to convey His Word to me. I would listen to messages and Bible verses, but I couldn't relate to them. I thought I was pursuing God, but in all reality, I was pursuing the traditions of the church. I became dead inside.

Life without the Word of God is death. Life becomes meaningless. I became powerless without Him. The Word of God brings life with meaning and motivates us to pursue Him. The more I read His Word, the more I wanted to know Him—to be in relationship with Him. I began to understand the meaning of my life and the purpose He created me for. It was in this little book that I found power and life. This book was leading me onto the path of destiny and became my survival guide in life.

> Oh, that my ways were directed to keep Your statutes!
> (Psalm 119:105)

I was pursuing religion without my survival guide. I wasn't on a pathway to destiny but a pathway to destruction. Even as saved

Christians, we can "do" religion. We may think that because we raise our hands to praise Him, pray the right prayers, listen to worship songs, and tithe that we are doing everything right in God's eyes. We get so caught up in the "ways" that we tend to forget the most important ingredient. Yes, life can get busy, but if we forget about our survival guide, life will be meaningless and powerless. Please understand that I'm not condemning anyone, but there is truth in what I'm saying, and we need to hear it. There is power, such power, in reading the Word of God! Hebrews 4:12 says,

> For the word of God *is* living and powerful, and sharper than any two-edged sword, piercing even to the division of soul and spirit, and of joints and marrow, and is a discerner of the thoughts and intents of the heart.

There's no healthy way to live life spiritually without the Word. We become surface Christians if we just skim the top of what God has for us. We need to go deeper than the surface. God is calling us to go deep. I can hear some of you saying right now, "But I don't have time. I can get what I need at Sunday service." God wants you to make the time. He wants to be the focus of your life. He wants to show you things. He wants to teach you.

There is power in His Word. Open up the book and see what He is saying to you. You can never reach your full potential of all you were created for without the power of His Word. You will never find your true pathway to destiny. The Word is essential to your life.

> All Scripture *is* given by inspiration of God, and *is* profitable for doctrine, for reproof, for correction, for instruction in righteousness, that the man of God may be complete, thoroughly equipped for every good work. (2 Timothy 3:16-17)

So what am I saying here? It's important to know the difference between having a "religious mindset" vs. having a mindset set on

CHAPTER 3: DISORDERLY CONDUCT

relationship with the Father. He is longing for you to have a relationship with Him. He wants you to get to know Him and hunger for His ways, not man-made ways.

Pursuit of Freedom

What does freedom feel like? When you are truly set free from something, you feel like you have the power to do anything set in front of you. You want to let out a loud whoop for joy! That's how I felt once I understood that I needed to be set free from having a religious spirit. It means that I didn't want to be blinded anymore by traditions or religious practices. As I read more and more of His Word and tried to understand it, I found myself growing closer and closer to my heavenly Father. Jesus was becoming so real to me through His Word. I didn't want to know about anything else. My relationship with Him became intimate like it was just Him and me—nobody else. I started to care less and less about the religious practices I had learned as a little boy. I knew they were meaningless and without power.

> **My church experience became so much more meaningful once I knew that there was more beyond the walls of the church.**

He is the true way to finding life with meaning and power. There was a new pursuit in my heart to be set free from the chains that bound me from truly knowing Him. My church experience became so much more meaningful once I knew that there was more beyond the walls of the church. Traditions of the church didn't bother me anymore because I knew who I was in Him. I knew I had the freedom to go directly to Him as a son, knowing that He would provide everything I needed through His Word and my relationship with Him. You have the freedom to pursue Him and only Him. Break away from religious mindsets and set your heart on Him. God is so good!

Danger Zone

We are all familiar with rules. If you live in any country in the world, you have a set of rules or laws you have to abide by. Most households are run by rules. I personally don't know of any household where a family member can do what they want when they want. My wife and I have responsibilities. We work, pay bills, do household chores, raise our children, etc. My children have responsibilities and expectations too. I have set boundaries and rules for their own good. I want them to be respectful of the rules, and I expect them to obey them. Rules and laws are made to keep us protected and safe.

So what does this mean for our spiritual walk with the Lord? *Legalism* is a term that means "strict conformity to law."[1] Legalism today is considered to be an excessive thing. When we think about laws or rules in the church, we can sometimes cross a fine line. We already have touched on traditions, which can be a form of legalism. Think about it. If you went to a church that has a rigid schedule of taking communion every Sunday and you suggest that maybe they could do once a month instead, how do you think they would react? My guess is that they wouldn't take it very well. Their mindset is set on taking communion every Sunday because they think, *That's the way it's always been done.*

> Beware lest anyone cheat you through philosophy and empty deceit, according to the tradition of men, according to the basic principles of the world, and not according to Christ. (Colossians 2:8)

The problem with this is that you begin to forget the real reason behind taking communion. It becomes a repetitive ritual with no value. Why do we take communion, and who is it for? Legalistic thinking can

---

1. *Webster's Collegiate Dictionary*, s.v. "legalism," (G. & C. Merriam Co., Springfield, MA: 1913).

Chapter 3: Disorderly Conduct

be a danger zone. It becomes personal. People get offended because "it's not the way" or it's not what they believe in. We can't force others to follow "our" set of rules or laws because we deem them to be right. If my friend decides he wants to get a tattoo, he has every right to get a tattoo without me lecturing him about my values on the subject. He has free will to do what he wants. I may not like tattoos, but it becomes legalistic when I try to press my views and opinions on him. I can't get mad at him because he doesn't agree with my views.

> Therefore, if you died with Christ from the basic principles of the world, why, as *though* living in the world, do you subject yourselves to regulations—"Do not touch, do not taste, do not handle," which all concern things which perish with the using—according to the commandments and doctrines of men? These things indeed have an appearance of wisdom in self-imposed religion, *false* humility, and neglect of the body, *but are* of no value against the indulgence of the flesh. (Colossians 2:20-23)

There are topics that get touchy among believers: how people raise their children, where we shop, what we drink, what version of the Bible is best, who our friends are, and I can go on and on; these are all things we need to be careful of in our walk with God.

It is not up to us to exert holiness on others. What they do is between them and God. That goes beyond people's individual lives to church bodies as well. We need to stay focused on what truly matters and stay out of the danger zone. Second Corinthians 3:17 tells us, "Now the Lord is the Spirit; and where the Spirit of the Lord *is*, there *is* liberty."

What truly matters? Jesus is what matters. We can show our love, but it can get dangerous if we start to demand that others think or act like us. We should only be thinking and acting like Jesus. That is why He created us—to be like Him.

Family Time

As we have already discussed, religious and legalistic mindsets can really throw a wrench in our walk with God and spiritual growth. These mindsets cannot only affect ourselves but can affect members of our households. We can sometimes create walls within our family structure that were not meant to be built. Because of how we think or act, we may be putting up barriers that may have lifetime effects on our family members.

> Because of how we think or act, we may be putting up barriers that may have lifetime effects on our family members.

What do I mean by this? When we impose our unhealthy mindsets on someone else, it can have a negative effect. We may think we mean well, but in reality, we are only pushing them away. We may come across as condemning or incite fear into them if they do not think or act like you. For example, we may give the impression that nothing is ever good enough. We may tell someone they are going to hell because of something they said or did (imposing fear) or that they must not really be saved. We may try to control or manipulate situations because we want our own way. Sometimes we rule with an iron fist. We tend to forget that everyone has free will to make their own choices and decisions for their life.

Our Father does not want to see us imprisoned. When we impose our unhealthy mindsets onto our loved ones, we are not living by His ways, which are created out of love. His ways do not condemn or bring fear. It all begins with us internally. God will bring things to our attention that He wants to deal within us.

This is a very important topic we need to cover, and please hear me when I say that I'm not saying this in a condemning way. My intention

Chapter 3: Disorderly Conduct

is to show you how these things can bring unintentional wounds. God wants to heal and restore you so you can walk into the fullness of what He has for you. He wants to not only see you restored, but He wants to see healing within the family unit and restoration to what He originally intended for us. He wants to see you set free from the bondage within you, and He wants to break down the barriers within your family. He is waiting for you to start demolition on the walls within you. He will be with you every step of the way because He is an awesome and loving Father. His desire is to bring joy and happiness back because He is that good. Yes, He is good!

God Is First, What Comes Next?

We have mentioned a few things previously that have caused a serious disorder in the body of Christ. As we see ourselves getting through these barriers, our journey takes us to another roadblock.

Once we begin to move forward out of legalism and religious mindsets, we tend to pick up some speed along the way. Before we know it, we're cruising the spiritual highway, and everything seems to be in the right place, especially our relationship with Father God. We begin to develop our spiritual gifts, and are eager to learn new things. We start to realize that we have a call on our lives to minister.

As this call becomes evident, our zeal and passion for what God has placed on our lives springs forth. Before we know it, we are up and running, full-speed ahead. Little by little, you are fully consumed by your calling.

Imagine watching a race car speeding on a racetrack. The car is going at max speed, and you look ahead and see something stuck on the racetrack. You are jumping up and down, waving your arms, trying to get the driver's attention so they don't crash. That's how it is for us sometimes. We don't see the debris ahead on the track because we are going full speed and are focused on the finish line. There may be people in your life who can see the racetrack and tell you to slow down and to be watchful of what is ahead. They are speaking into your life and giving you wisdom. During these times, we need to stop and listen.

The King's Bridal Company

What is God saying? When all the commotion dies down, we are able to hear things we couldn't hear before because we were so caught up in our call or ministry.

Maybe there is a knocking on your heart. Who could be there? Maybe a loved one, such as a spouse or child who has been knocking, but you've been too busy to hear. You get so wrapped up in your ministry that you forget the ministry of your own family. Our lives can become so busy that we get caught up in what we are doing, and our loved ones get left behind. I'm not saying we should stop ministering, but we need to find a healthy balance between God, our calling, and our family.

> For if a man does not know how to rule his own
> house, how will he take care of the church of God?
> (1 Timothy 3:5)

Yes, we should always put God ahead of everything else, but what comes next? We need to make sure our calling doesn't become who we are or put our identity in our ministry rather than in Jesus. We need to take care of our families. God wants us to do His will, but He also wants us to make sure our families are emotionally and spiritually secure. After all, remember that we are establishing a legacy, and we need to honor the legacy God has given us. We should attend to our spouses and children above everyone else we are trying to help.

There are going to be times when we get busy. I get that; I've been there. But at the same time, we have to learn something very important. For some of us, this may be very difficult. There are three words everyone should learn to abide by: "Just say no!" Yup! You got it; learn to say no!

I can't tell you how many stories I've heard from people (including myself) where we regret getting caught up in something we wish we hadn't. It's also a good idea to ask God what He thinks you should do before committing to anything.

My wife especially has a difficult time with this. She has such a loving heart that she has a hard time telling people no when they ask her to do something. She has learned many lessons by not saying no

Chapter 3: Disorderly Conduct

to people or not asking God first what He thinks she should do. Once, she was so excited to get asked to do a project for someone that she wholeheartedly committed before asking God what He thought. It sounded promising, and she ignored all the bells and whistles (Warning! Danger Ahead!) going off in her head at the time. She went full-steam ahead, and within weeks regretted the decision she had made.

Because she is an honorable person, Kristine stayed true to her word and finished the project. It turned out to be different than she thought it would be and ended up being a source of major stress in her life. The project took long hours, and it took away from her family life. She began to feel guilty because the project also began to take away her time with the Lord. Our God is so loving and good. He sees everything, and He knew my wife's heart. He knew she wasn't doing this for herself. It was a good learning experience for her in many ways. God used that experience to show her the gifts He had stored up for her. God would have eventually shown her these gifts that were inside of her, but He used something that disheartened her for something good. Her disappointment turned into a blessing!

This is my point. Don't get too wrapped up in your call or ministry that you forget the main purpose of why you have a call and a ministry. Don't forget your first love, Jesus. Don't forget what comes next, and that is the love of family. God will always make sure you have time for ministry. Make sure you ask Him to show you how to steward it right so your family doesn't get the short end of the stick.

Chapter 4: Childish Delights

I don't know about you, but when I was a little kid, Christmas was my favorite time of the year. Once the snow started flying in Pennsylvania, thoughts of Christmas presents started floating around in my head. I would get my paper and pencil and start making my Christmas list. Back then, I didn't have the Internet to look at endless websites for all the things I wanted. I had to wait for the store flyers and catalogs to arrive in the mail. Saturday morning cartoons would be full of the latest fad commercials to target their young audience, and whatever hooked my fancy that year would make the list.

As I got older, my list would reflect the stage in my life. So what am I getting at here about my Christmas list? You got it! Gifts! We all love to get gifts. Birthdays are another special day where gifts are given. You don't have to be a kid to like gifts. I still get excited when a gift is handed to me. Gifts are not only exciting for the receiver but the giver too. As a parent, I love giving gifts to my children. Seeing their exuberant faces and shouts of delight is priceless. It brings back memories of myself as a child and the feelings of joy and happiness as I opened the gift.

Speaking of receiving gifts, let me tell you about an incredible encounter I once had with the Holy Spirit. I was caught up in the Spirit and was taken on a glorious joy ride. I love it when the Holy Spirit does that. I felt so carefree as I was soaring through the sky. I came upon the most beautiful, purest of white flowers. I reached my hand out to touch them, and suddenly right before my eyes, the flowers transformed into a gorgeous dove. It was so intense that it took my breath away. I then started to fly toward a mountain. The feeling was so exhilarating as the Holy Spirit whisked me up the side of the mountain right to the top. When I got to the top, I saw a snow-white, spotless lamb. Our eyes immediately locked, and then the lamb turned and walked into a tent. Something within the tent was drawing me in. What I saw next was so astonishing that I gasped in amazement. Jesus walked out of the tent, holding something in His hands. He looked straight at me and reached out to hand me a box—a gift. My hands stretched forward to receive the gift, and then I was back on my bed. The joy I felt at that moment was indescribable.

> Every good gift and every perfect gift is from above, and comes down from the Father of lights, with whom there is no variation or shadow of turning. (James 1:17)

Imagine Father God's face when He gives us a gift. There are many spiritual gifts our Father can give us. Every believer is given gifts. I believe He delights in such joy and happiness just knowing we decided to receive His gift. Think about your emotion as you give a person a gift you know they will love. That's how our Father is when He gives us a gift He knows we will love and cherish. It brings Him pleasure to make us happy!

What happens when you receive a gift you love? Your immediate reaction is to give the person who gave you the gift a hug because you are so thankful. Our Father is waiting for us to run to Him and hug Him. He doesn't give us gifts so we can love Him back; He gives us gifts because He loves us. It's that simple. He always wants to give us good things, whether it is a word to bring comfort, a thought to help us move forward, or a dream to give us insight into a particular situation.

Let's take a look at the spiritual gifts mentioned in scripture. As we do this, it's not my intention to break down every gift and show you how they each function. My intention is to give you an awareness of the giftings as a whole and why they are used amongst the body of Christ.

Chapter 4: Childish Delights

> Now concerning spiritual *gifts,* brethren, I do not want you to be ignorant: You know that you were Gentiles, carried away to these dumb idols, however you were led. Therefore I make known to you that no one speaking by the Spirit of God calls Jesus] accursed, and no one can say that Jesus is Lord except by the Holy Spirit. There are diversities of gifts, but the same Spirit. There are differences of ministries, but the same Lord. And there are diversities of activities, but it is the same God who works all in all. But the manifestation of the Spirit is given to each one for the profit *of all:* for to one is given the word of wisdom through the Spirit, to another the word of knowledge through the same Spirit, to another faith by the same Spirit, to another gifts of healings by the same Spirit, to another the working of miracles, to another prophecy, to another discerning of spirits, to another *different* kinds of tongues, to another the interpretation of tongues. But one and the same Spirit works all these things, distributing to each one individually as He wills. (1 Corinthians 12:1-11)

We must keep in mind that the spiritual gifts are given from the Spirit of God and are manifested to bring His glory. The gifts of the Holy Spirit demonstrate His supernatural power through us for both the unbeliever and believer. The manifestation of the gifts are used to strengthen and equip the body of Christ to bring an awareness of His glory—the full expression of His love for us.

The gifts given by the Spirit of God are truly amazing. If we're not careful, we can misuse them for what God intended for us. They are very powerful, and just like anything else that holds power, they must be handled with care and stewarded properly. 1 Peter 4:10 says, "As each one has received a gift, minister it to one another, as good stewards of the manifold grace of God." The gifts are used to manifest God's glory, and if used inappropriately, they can really mess things up on both personal and corporate levels.

When we receive gifts from the Holy Spirit, responsibility comes with it. Unlike earthly treasures where they fade away and get old or broken, gifts from the Father never break, never go away, or get old. And no matter what happens in your spiritual growth (you may get stuck or backslide), you never lose your gifts. "For God's gifts and his call can never be withdrawn." (Romans 11:29 NLT). They will always be with you. Our Father is so good He will never expect them to be given back. God knows we will fumble the ball at the goal line. We may drop the ball, but the good news is that He also knows our hearts. It's part of our learning curve on our journey of spiritual growth. We will get into this more later in the book.

Let's get back to how good God is. As I discussed already, God is so good. When He gives, He gives. The Lord wants us to grow and fully mature into the fullness of what He destined for us. When He gives us spiritual gifts, they can sometimes be fun to use. Think about it. When God gives us gifts, they are supernatural gifts. We cannot use these gifts on our own accord, so when we get them, we may be surprised at what we can do. We might say, "Hey! Look at what I can do!" Remember, our gifts should be used out of love for one another. They were not given just for us, but also given to us for others. When you grasp this point, you start to see an entirely different outlook on your gifts and your walk of destiny.

Occupational Hazard

We've all taken risks of some sort. A risk is when you take a chance that something may or may not cause harm or loss. It could be dangerous. There are different types of risks. People risk their lives every day in this world. We take a risk every time we get in a car. Some people take risks with their finances or businesses. Have you ever had a job with an occupational hazard? You've taken some sort of risk as a result of the job. Most work environments will give training to help protect you from the hazards or risks of the job. Safety should always come first.

We don't really think about it, but when we use our God-given gifts, we can think of them as an occupational hazard. You have to be careful

Chapter 4: Childish Delights

when using spiritual gifts because they can be risky if not used properly. We should all proceed with caution and have a "safety first" mindset.

If we're not careful how we use our spiritual gifts, it can become a dangerous situation. It can be like a time bomb about to go off. Spiritual gifts could be destructive if not used in the way God intended. The gifts cannot only be a danger to others but to ourselves too. We need to be careful not to manipulate or abuse our gifts because it will only lead us down a path to destruction.

Spiritual gifts could be destructive if not used in the way God intended.

Pride can easily set in when using the gifts. I can't tell you how many meetings or services I have been in when someone yells out (very loudly), "Thus saith the Lord!" and gives a prophetic word because they want to be the center of attention. They may say something hurtful, like, "God wants you to know you shouldn't be hanging around those people anymore because they are bad for you!" First of all, we need to honor the house or place of worship we are in. We should always go to leadership before giving a prophetic word unless they know you and have given you the authority to speak freely. Secondly, if God is telling you something about someone, always remember that it should not be done in a condemning way. Our God is not in the business of condemnation.

> For God did not send His Son into the world to condemn the world, but that the world through Him might be saved. (John 3:17)

Spiritual gifts should not be used out of order. When things are out of order, it creates chaos. God is not about chaos. We need to remember to be respectful of how we use our gifts.

I cannot reiterate enough that the supernatural gifts are given by God to you. These gifts represent Him, not you. As we use our gifts, we are representing God within us, not ourselves and the "look at me!" complex. How can we know if we are using the gifts properly? It comes down to one word: love.

The first thing to remember is that love is the number one factor in desiring a gift from God. After all, love is the greatest gift (1 Corinthians 13). If you don't use your gift in love, then it will destroy you. Love is amazing. Love is greatness. Love is adoration. Love is affection. Love is tenderness, warmth, and passion. The gifts should be used out of love for God, which leads you to love people. Without love, it will just be about you. Functioning in love not only honors God but also gives respect and honor to others. When this happens, others will see God in you. They will not only see the outpouring of love within you, but they will experience it!

Using your spiritual gifts can be risky business. Is that a risk you're willing to take? I know I'm willing to risk it all for my King Jesus. The gifts are given to help and lift up others. As long as you're walking in love and representing your Father, the Holy Spirit will guide you and walk along with you.

Thrill of the Ride

Have you ever felt a rush? It's that moment when your heart rate increases, and you feel a surge of energy or excitement. For some people, they live for the thrill. They are always looking for the next big rush. It could be skydiving, rock climbing, or white-water rafting. For me, it's amusement park rides. I love that rushing feeling as my adrenaline kicks in. My favorite is roller coaster rides with steep drops. I love putting my hands in the air and letting the rush take over. It is such an exhilarating feeling.

As God reveals gifts to us, it can be exhilarating. I remember the time when my wife had desired one of the spiritual gifts. We had been praying and asking God for revelation, and we believed that in His time, the gift would come. On the day she received the gift, she could not

Chapter 4: Childish Delights

contain her excitement. She was like a little girl who just received the best present ever! I remember her joy and excitement as she was telling me all about the encounter she had with the Holy Spirit. She was so amazed by this beautiful gift and so full of sweet emotion. We both glorified Him for letting her unwrap this desirous, precious gift. He is such a good Father and so full of love for His children. He wants to give us the desires of our hearts.

> Pursue love, and desire spiritual *gifts,* but especially that you may prophesy. (1 Corinthians 14:1)

In our exhilaration, we have to remember to honor the giver and not the gifts. We need to be humble before Him. We do not live for the gifts; we live for Him. As I mentioned before, as long as we walk in love, represent Him in what we say and how we act, and give Him all the honor and glory, we will be blessed beyond measure. People will see Him in us and want what we have. They will want Jesus. They will want to be closer to Him and have a relationship with Him. That is His heart's desire; to have a relationship with us so we can grow and learn in Him. That relationship will lead us to the destiny that lies ahead for us.

One thing that's important to mention here is that our gifts are unique to each of us. Every one of us is specifically designed in God's eyes. He knew us before we were even born!

> Before I formed you in the womb I knew you; before you were born I sanctified you; I ordained you a prophet to the nations. (Jeremiah 1:5)

He knew if we were going to be a gifted singer, a talented artist, or a smart business person. Let's face it. We are not all gifted singers (I do my best, but I usually am singing off-key), and I certainly am no Michelangelo! As with natural talents or gifts, our spiritual gifts are specifically given to us by God. I would love to be a better singer or a talented artist, but I am not and nor will I ever be. God didn't make me that way. Imagine if we were all made with the same talents and gifts, and everyone could do whatever they wanted in this life. There would be extreme competition amongst ourselves, which would result in chaos and confusion. That's not God's intention. And He certainly is not about confusion. He has everything planned out so the talents and gifts are spread out, and every area is covered. It is quite amazing if you actually think about it!

We should never desire other's spiritual gifts or try to be something we are not. We should never seek the thrill because it looks and sounds exhilarating. Our heart needs to be in the right place when we seek and desire spiritual gifts. Each and every one of us on this earth has a spiritual gift, it's what helps makes us who we are.

God gives His gifts for us to unwrap in His timing. Keep seeking and desiring, and He will reveal *your* special gifts to you!

> For I wish that all men were even as I myself. But each one has his own gift from God, one in this manner and another in that. (1 Corinthians 7:7)

Front and Center

Do you remember when you were a kid and you heard the words, "The circus is coming to town?" Our heads would be filled with elephants, tigers, monkeys, and flying acrobats. My mouth is watering right now just thinking about the popcorn and cotton candy! I remember as a kid counting down the days until the circus came. It was a big deal back then.

The circus is all about performance and entertainment. According to a famous American circus company, their circus was considered "The Greatest Show on Earth." If you've ever been to the circus, you know how captivating and thrilling it can be. The moment the lights came on, your attention was captivated, and a stirring of excitement deep within you took hold. It is truly amazing how trained animal acts and daring performances of human skill can cause such a commotion within us.

Chapter 4: Childish Delights

Just like the great show of the circus can grab our attention, so can the supernatural. As I said before, the gifts of the Holy Spirit are amazing and awesome. They need to be stewarded correctly because when used improperly, they can really cause a disorder in the body of Christ.

> Let all things be done decently and in order.
> (1 Corinthians 14:40).

It is important to understand that it's one thing if God is bringing the show, but an entirely different thing if we are trying to be the star of the show. There is only one star, and that is Jesus Himself. He may use us to show Himself, but we need to remember that it is all about Him and His love for us.

> For of Him and through Him and to Him *are* all things,
> to whom *be* glory forever. Amen. (Romans 11:36)

In today's modern era of church, we have lights, cameras, and action. That is a fact in today's western society. Add a worship team, and boom, you got yourself a great event. Don't get me wrong. I love a great event, but if our hearts are not centered on King Jesus, then we remove the awe out of focusing on Him. After all, the event is supposed to bring glory to Him. When the event starts to remove the attention off of Him to focus on other things, then there's a problem.

Now let's add another ingredient to the recipe. We have lights, cameras, action, and worship. Add giftings as the icing on the cake, and you have the perfect recipe for a great event. God is so good that He wants to give us a great time. He wants to grab our attention. He wants our mouths to water in thirst and hunger for Him. He wants us to glorify His Son, King Jesus. I'm not saying that our intentions are not focused on Him, but sometimes circumstances can cause us to take our gaze off of Him.

In my own experience, I've managed to watch my giftings become front and center like a ringmaster at a circus instead of Jesus being front and center. Remember, He uses us to show Himself, not for us to showcase ourselves. I had to repent and ask for forgiveness.

How did it happen? What happened? Well, for starters, all the attention was on me. My giftings became an idol to me because when I "performed," all attention came to me. I began to idolize or put my gifts before God rather than put God first. Think about how easy it is to get caught up in the attention. It's all happened to us one way or another in one aspect of life, whether it be us or someone else. It could be within our own families, our jobs, or our church life. For myself, I am a "words-of-affirmation" guy. That is my love language. That's what does it for me! With that said, there were times in my life where I wasn't strong in my identity of being a child of God. The gifting became my focus, and people would lift me up and affirm what I was doing. I would then have a tendency to focus on the gift and not His face. Because of the attention, pride and arrogance crept in.

If we're not careful, this can happen with the supernatural. Others may see it within us, and because of pride, we have a hard time looking within ourselves to see it. I was completely out of balance. Visions, dreams, and spiritual encounters became my focus. When the experiences didn't happen, or I didn't get a prophetic word for a church or person, I thought I must have done something wrong. I thought I must have been in sin, and of course, at times without being able to see it, pride was a culprit of that.

> By pride comes nothing but strife, but with the well-advised *is* wisdom. (Proverbs 13:10)

God is so good that He allowed me to make mistakes so I could learn. I had to learn that without Him, I am nothing. How did I eventually see it? Through healing and deliverance. As we talked about in the previous chapters on healing and deliverance, I had to come to the end of myself and die to self (let go of my selfish, worldly ways) so I could see clearly. I was functioning in my flesh rather than functioning in the Spirit.

CHAPTER 4: CHILDISH DELIGHTS

> And those *who are* Christ's have crucified the flesh with its passions and desires. If we live in the Spirit, let us also walk in the Spirit. (Galatians 5:24-25)

I had to learn to lean on Him instead of my own understanding. Before any healing took place, I was spiritually blinded and couldn't see what I was doing. The Lord pointed out to me that my identity was based on performance and not relationship. I would go from one experience to the next and focus on my gift, not my giver (Jesus). I am very cautious of that trap, even today, because, as I said before, pride is always lurking at the door—especially when it comes to power gifts and offices. Be on alert! Take time and go in your secret place with the Lord and learn to evaluate your walk in ministry. Ask God to reveal the things He wants you to see and work on in your life.

Pride is always lurking at the door— especially when it comes to power gifts and offices.

It's perfectly okay to go to a performance as long as Jesus is front and center and the Holy Spirit is performing the show while the Father is overseeing it. Let's not get caught up in ourselves. We have a tendency to get in the way of what God wants to do. By learning to remove ourselves from front and center, we will find the true front and center of God Himself.

What's Up with Titles Anyway?

Titles, titles, titles. It is what our identity is based on in the world system. Think about every time you have to fill out a form of some sort. What is the first thing they ask you? What your "title" is (Mr., Mrs., Ms.).

How important are titles, and how useful are they? For starters, it's useful to know if someone is a doctor, they have a title. If you live in another country, for example, and someone is born of nobility, they will have a title (prince, princess, duke, duchess, etc.). How about principal or coach? If you are in the military, you have a title. Most titles are earned. You don't just wake up one day as a principal of a school, captain of the Navy, or chief surgeon at a hospital. It takes hard work and usually some sort of training to earn a title. Even if you inherit a title, you still have to have training to know what duties you're responsible for.

Growing up in a family business has its advantages and disadvantages. There are times when we can make our own hours or come and go as we please. When my stomach starts to growl, telling me it's lunchtime, I can just hop in my car and go get lunch. Doctor appointment? No problem! It also has its downside too. If we're on a big job and there is a schedule to be met, then we have to make sure we are putting in the hours to finish the job on time. Some days I have spent putting in an enormous amount of hours just to make sure I finish a job within the timeframe given to the customer. I have even put in extended hours on weekends when I should have been home with my family. Running a local business is all about making the customer happy because our business is mostly run on word of mouth. If we do a good job and please a customer, they will return for more business and tell others about us.

For most of the outside world looking in at us, everything looks like peaches and cream. They think that because you are a business owner, you have nice cars, nice houses, and you can take vacations whenever and wherever you want because you are your own boss. People don't see the reality of owning your own business. They don't see the bills that pile up. They don't understand that building up assets in a business can take time and money. Most people do not think of the debt that accumulates at times, and they certainly have no clue how it can affect family relationships. Responsibility for people who work for you is also a huge weight to carry on your shoulders. Believe me when I say it is no walk in the park!

Besides all that, I liked being in charge and being my own boss. I may sound a bit arrogant here, but I had to learn some things in my life to realize what a jerk I had become. Being a boss's son when I was a

Chapter 4: Childish Delights

teen starting out in the family business gave me a sense of authority. Yes, my dad was hard on me at times, and I had to learn some things, but I also got away with stuff that the other workers couldn't get away with. My dad wanted me to succeed in the business. He knew that someday I would be taking over and running the business myself. He was teaching me as I went along. He let me do things my way at times, knowing they were not good decisions (he would always let me know his opinion and give me advice first). But guess what? I was a know-it-all and wouldn't listen and wanted to do things on my own, my way. When I did things my way, they usually didn't turn out so good. You see, my dad knew a lot of things about how to run the business successfully; I was still learning. I can look back now and appreciate that he let me make mistakes so I can see what I did wrong and learn from it.

What are you trying to say here, Sal? Well, for starters, I became arrogant and prideful because I had been given authority. Because my dad allowed me to do what I wanted and learn from the business, I didn't take the learning experience seriously. At that time, I didn't appreciate how much he loved me and wanted me to succeed in the business. I only thought about my entitlement as a business owner's son. I was very immature. I walked around thinking I had a position of authority and acted like a king of my domain at times. That position of authority went straight to my head! It wasn't good in so many ways. I was a prideful, selfish jerk who thought the only thing that mattered was little old me. I do not like to admit that during this time in my life, I didn't even care about my employees' lives. If something didn't benefit me, then I didn't care! I can honestly say that I'm not proud of that season in my life.

As it turned out, things were not all peaches and cream during that time. The Lord was trying to get my attention. Why? Because I meant something to Him, and He loved me. He looked beyond my faults and saw the greatness in me and what I was to become. Just like my earthly father, my heavenly Father let me make mistakes so I could learn from them. The Lord had a plan for my life, just like He has a plan for you. Plans don't just happen overnight. There is a process. In this process, we learn how to walk with the Lord. We learn to trust and have faith in

Him. We learn to listen and follow His ways. We learn what to do and what not to do. We learn how to be like Him. We learn how to walk in the authority He has given us.

Let me fast-forward a bit here. The Lord got my attention, and I accepted Him as my Lord and Savior. Unfortunately, I still was a prideful, arrogant jerk. How did that happen? Because I didn't really know who I was. I didn't know my identity in Christ. I didn't know what it meant to truly be His son in the kingdom. Yeah, I was His son in His family business, and maybe that went a little to my head. Let me tell you what happened. I learned that I was called to ministry shortly after I was saved. This sounded amazing to my ears. Not only did I get to serve the Lord, but it came with a position. Soon after I started attending church, I was asked to be a deacon. I gladly accepted the position, and it wasn't long before I was asked to move to the position of the youth leader. That was awesome because it gave me the opportunity to do what I love—preach.

The next season of my life brought me to a new church, and I began to attend ministry school. I was soon asked to be on staff and be one of the pastors at church. I became controlling and legalistic. At times I was obnoxious and felt entitled. I thought I knew everything because I knew some scripture. The fact of the matter is when it came to positional authority; I completely misinterpreted who I was supposed to be representing, King Jesus. My identity was in my position, not the King. I was seeking attention for myself when in reality, I should have been seeking my Lord and Savior, Jesus Christ. I can look back now and see where I went wrong. I was wrapped up in my titles and authority. I was directing myself on my journey through life rather than letting my Father direct my steps.

So how did I get through it? God allowed me to look in the mirror and see the real me. I saw the obnoxious, prideful, arrogant, controlling, legalistic, selfish, entitled jerk. Wow! Did I really say that right? Yes, I was that person. I am not that same man today, and I thank my Lord for showing me the way. I was in an inner prison and was chained up, crying to be set free. Things became one big ball of mess in my life. Our

CHAPTER 4: CHILDISH DELIGHTS

Father is so good. I can't say that enough! As I said before, He wants to see us set free from all our turmoils. I was walking around with a big ego and a big head. It was just a matter of time before I imploded. God redirected my steps toward finding healing and deliverance.

> "For I will restore health to you and heal you of your wounds," says the Lord, "Because they called you an outcast saying: 'This is Zion; no one seeks her.'" (Jeremiah 30:17)

To this day, I am so thankful that He opened my eyes and ears so I could hear Him calling out to me. He brought people into my life to help me along the way. God will do that. He will bring people into your life to help direct your steps. And never did anyone come up to me and say, "Hey Sal, you're a big jerk, and you need help!" They might have wanted to, but God needed to get my attention. God will show you these things because He is the only one who can release the healing and deliverance needed to make you whole again. He brought an amazing counselor into my life who lovingly showed me the error of my ways. I needed to see the errors first within myself before I could move forward. I knew they were there, but I needed to *want* to change into a better me. In all reality, it's God who reveals the things in your life that need to change, and it's up to you to want to deal with them.

> **In all reality, it's God who reveals the things in your life that need to change, and it's up to you to want to deal with them.**

In ministry, we need to be careful not to let the titles get to our heads. It can be easy to let pride settle in. I've seen it happen to so many good people. When titles are given out freely, sometimes it's before we are ready to receive or walk in those titles, just like when I was a teenager in my dad's business, and I thought I knew it all. I was just a kid and had many things to learn first before I could really receive the authority to successfully run the business. Even though I made mistakes, I didn't learn from them because of the pride within myself. It blinded me from being teachable or accepting criticism with love. It was the same for me when I was newly saved and received titles and authority before I knew who I really was in Christ Jesus. I was like a kid again and had many things to learn and go through before God could release the authority in me.

God is the one who authorizes when it is time to give out the authority, not us. And when it is time, God will give us the training manual to show us how to walk in authority with love and grace. Jesus was our prime example. Seek Him and His face, and you will know when the time is right to boldly step out.

Chapter 5: Unfinished Business

As you take the journey of seeing yourself for who you truly are in Jesus and learning to let go of those things that are holding you back, a new you will begin to emerge. You start to see the old ways pass, and the new things spring forth.

> Therefore, if anyone *is* in Christ, *he is* a new creation; old things have passed away; behold, all things have become new. (2 Corinthians 5:17)

Pain, tears, and sadness become a thing of the past because now you begin to see HIM. You start to gaze and become awestruck. You realize that without Him, things are hopeless. You need Him; you crave Him and His presence. He is all things good. Your approach to life and your perspective have changed. You begin to see people through a different lens, and your attitudes toward them changes. You are full of love. You might have once condemned people who didn't believe in Jesus because you were saved and had all the answers. You think to yourself, "Who is this person I am becoming? I think I like the new me!"

As you look at yourself in the mirror, you see a change. You feel a new sense of freedom because God is working in you, bringing hidden things to the surface so you can deal with them. At this stage in your journey, you realize that there might be some unfinished business that still needs taking care of.

The King's Bridal Company

As we stay on the road to destiny, hitting some potholes along the way or maybe driving off the road at times, our Lord has continuously shined His light upon our path.

> The Lord, He *is* the One who goes before you. He will be with you, He will not leave you nor forsake you; do not fear nor be dismayed. (Deuteronomy 31:8)

He continues to remind us how amazing we are, that He chose us before the foundations of the earth and that we are called to represent Him in our lifetime. We don't even realize the moments when He picks us up and carries us. Truth be told, this road to divine destiny is not always a smooth one. There will be some doubt, and we will face adversity, but remember this: if God sees that we truly want to stay on that road, then He will do everything in His power to sustain us. He will see us through. We don't need to fear that we will crash and burn.

As destiny continues to dream for you and calls you out, rest assured that something is going to pop up that we will have to deal with. Look at it like this: you are building a brand new house—your dream house. You want everything to go smoothly and perfectly as it is being built. I'm in construction, and I can honestly say that I have never come across a project that went smoothly and perfectly. There was always something that came up or a snag here and there, even if it was something that was easily fixed. One thing is for sure; I never left anything unfinished. I always tried to fix the problem.

It is like us on our journey. We are the houses, and God is building us up as we follow Him. He shows us the problems so we can fix them. He wants the perfect house. He wants to purify us. He created us to be like Him.

Our house should look like His house. It is a magnificent, glorious house. It is your dream house! Just like in the natural, you would never want to leave your dream house unfinished because you wouldn't fulfill your dream. In the spiritual, God is looking to perfect your dream house. He doesn't want you to leave it unfinished. As you are building your

Chapter 5: Unfinished Business

house, there just might be some unfinished business that may cause you to stumble along the way.

> The Lord will perfect *that which* concerns me; Your mercy, O Lord, *endures* forever; do not forsake the works of Your hands. (Psalm 138:8)

It's a Busy, Busy, World

We live in a hectic world. Everything is becoming faster and more efficient, but people still want things NOW! Everyone seems to be losing patience these days. I am guilty of that too. That is one thing in my life that I continuously work on: patience. There never seems to be enough time in the day to accomplish everything. I feel like that all the time. I get up in the morning and plan my day, making a mental list of all the things I need to get done. At the end of the day, I feel like I've accomplished nothing because I didn't do everything I wanted to do. Sound familiar? Most of the time we are running, running, running—but instead of moving forward, we are spinning our wheels. We need to stop spinning our wheels, take a break, and relax. Give God a moment. How many of us truly give time for God in our daily schedules? Our worlds are spinning, and we think to ourselves, *I barely have time for myself, let alone anything else!*

We pack our daily schedules with "to do" lists. Our days are busy with family, jobs, chores, bills, appointments, and the list goes on and on. Then after a long day, dinner has to be on the table before we can finally settle down to watch some TV and relax. Oh, wait....now my bed is calling me! Yes, sleep! And the cycle begins all over again the next day.

My point is that we need to find time for God. We should be making Him a priority above all else. Try to make it a point in your day to focus on Him. Let your mind drift and seek His face. On this journey, it's so important to stay connected to the Father. He loves it! He craves it when you look to Him. It's in these precious moments that we will grow and mature in Him. He will speak to us. As we walk along with Him, we have to stay focused on the path before us.

Think about it like this. We always make time for our children. Why? Because relationships and nurturing are so important for their development. For them to mature and develop properly, they need love and attention. It's the same for us. We need a relationship with our heavenly Father to grow and mature spiritually.

I don't know about you, but when I spend quality time with my own children, I feel so great afterward. You will feel the same when you spend time with God. He will make you feel awesome. He will make you feel loved! Go to Him. Find time for Him. Be thankful for Him and all that He does for you. He will bless you beyond belief!

Knock, Knock! Who's There?

Have you ever looked back on your life and thought about all the things you have accomplished? Or have you looked ahead and wondered what will come next? Personally, I never would have imagined that God had a purpose for me in ministry. Over twenty years ago, I was bound in chains, running a family business, trying to make the next dollar, and hoping to retire at an early age. I look at my life now, and the only thing I care about is being bound to the Lord and living my life for Jesus. Here I am today, writing about His goodness and sharing my experiences. Since I have been saved, the desire to preach has intensified. Even though I have been ministering now for many years, the yearning to get out and preach about my Jesus has been a raging fire deep within my soul. The burning is increasing as we get closer to the day He returns or I see Him in heaven, whichever comes first.

Inside all of us, there is a burning that has flourished. The more you seek His face and want to know more about Him, the more intense the burning becomes. This cry or urgency to want more of Him just doesn't fade away. This is the Spirit of God within us. For the Word says that God's Spirit dwells in our midst (1 Corinthians 3:16).

CHAPTER 5: UNFINISHED BUSINESS

I want you to close your eyes for a minute and really think about that. The Spirit of the Living God lives within us. He actually chose us to take up residence. The thought of God's Spirit living inside of me blows my mind! Have you ever looked up in the sky on a starry night and thought about the vast universe? Or have you ever seen a picture of the solar system? I remember being in grade school and learning about the planets and being in complete shock at the size of the earth compared to the sun or other planets. When you put yourself in that perspective and how small we really are in this universe, it is mind-blowing what our Creator has accomplished for us. Think about our Almighty God and how awesome He is, and think about all of creation and all He's done, then realize that He chose to come live inside of us so we can represent Him and His kingdom. Wow!

The Spirit of God doesn't just come and take up residence within you. He wants to be invited.

How does it all begin? Well, for starters, the Spirit of God doesn't just come and take up residence within you. He wants to be invited. When you have someone over to your house, you invite them over. It would be weird to think that people can just come into your house without being welcomed or invited in at any time. It is the same with the Spirit of God. He wants you to welcome and invite Him in. He will not enter unless He is invited in, and He certainly will not go against your free will. He will not force Himself in. He is very gentle. As He knocks, His voice is calling you. He's like that friend who wants to come over and hang out. But instead of inviting Himself over, He calls you to see what you're up to, hoping you will say, "Hey! Whatcha doing? Want to come over and hang out?" You await His presence. You hear His knock and then His gentle voice. You open the door, and there He is, standing before you. You welcome Him in and ask Him to dine with you. It is glorious!

> Behold, I stand at the door and knock. If anyone hears My voice and opens the door, I will come in to him and dine with him, and he with Me. (Revelation 3:20)

Can you imagine dining with our Lord? It sounds so intimate and romantic. Sitting with our Lord and Savior, breaking bread. It brings such emotion just to think about sharing a meal with Him. But wait a minute. What if we missed the opportunity to sit and dine with Him? What if we missed the knocking? When the Spirit of God knocks, He doesn't come and bang loudly on our doors. Like I said before, it is a gentle knock. We are often so busy that we don't hear the knock. We get caught up in our lives, and the knock goes unnoticed. Unfortunately, we could be too busy in our ministry or the assignment God has placed on our lives to hear Him knocking. If we're not careful, we won't sense what God is saying to us, and our flesh will get the best of us. We need to be in tune with our spirit and what the Spirit of the Lord is saying to us.

Like we talked about in the previous section, take some time and listen for the Lord. He is so eager for you to open the door. He wants to sit and dine with you. He just wants to be with *you*. Soak in His presence. He wants to listen to your hurts and wipe away your tears. He wants to rejoice with you when things go well. Don't miss out. Hear the knock. Open the door. He's waiting.

Did You Call For a Bellhop?

Sunny skies and a warm, humid breeze hit me as the bellhop of the hotel opened my car door. He scurried to grab our baggage and then opened the door as my wife and I entered the hotel. After we checked in, he brought our bags up to our room and asked if there was anything else we needed.

That was a scene from when my wife and I went on our honeymoon. Honestly, it felt so good to have someone wait on me. It made me feel important—almost like a celebrity. Like I was somebody in this world and that someone actually cared about me. I didn't have to lift a finger.

Chapter 5: Unfinished Business

He knew what to do the moment we arrived in the car. It was like, "Here's Sal Cerra! Roll out the red carpet! Sound the trumpets!"

Okay, back to reality. Most of the time, I'm my own bellhop; I open my own doors and carry my own bags. That's not a bad thing in the natural world we live in. But what about spiritually? Most of us don't even think about opening our own doors in the spirit realm. I'm here to tell you that this is serious, and is something we need to be aware of and take caution with.

> The key of the house of David I will lay on his shoulder; so he shall open, and no one shall shut; and he shall shut, and no one shall open. (Isaiah 22:22)

Before I begin, let me tell you about a dream I had that was pretty serious. The Lord was speaking to me about ministry because I was in a place where I felt inpatient (Remember that I said I have a hard time with patience?). In the dream, I was on an airplane. I looked out the window and saw a huge house, like a mansion. I knew immediately whose house it was. The house belonged to a prominent author and evangelist from a megachurch. Suddenly, I felt the urge to turn around in my seat and I was shocked by who was sitting behind me—it was the well-known evangelist himself. To my astonishment, I heard him say, "Sal, who opens doors?" I responded by saying, "Jesus opens doors!" With a grin from ear to ear, he said, "Yes! And you already know that!" I woke up and knew immediately that the Lord was reminding me that He would be the One to open the doors for my ministry.

There are times when we hear knocking on doors in ministry, and we are eager to open them. I can say this firsthand because I have done it myself. It is a tough lesson to learn. Even if the knocking is not ministry-related, there's always some kind of knocking waiting for the door to be opened. It may be a business opportunity, friendships, new adventures, career choices, moves, etc. It can be any kind of knock, and these types of knocks are loud and untimely. They look great and sound wonderful, so we think, *I have to open the door because what is on the other side is going to be so awesome!*

An incredible opportunity may lie behind the door; however, it usually comes with a price and a lot of effort on your part. Those knocks are easier to hear because they are like "music to the ears." Typically the knock is so loud that it muffles the voice of the Holy Spirit. These are the doors most of us will open and later regret. We tend to open doors before the Lord says it is okay—and without knowing if He wants us to even open them at all. Have you ever heard the phrase "going before the timing of the Lord?" This is what I am talking about.

> ## When we open a door that was not in God's timing or plan for our life, it can result in disaster.

When we open a door that was not in God's timing or plan for our life, it can result in disaster. The good news is that God doesn't allow us to crash and burn but uses our bad choices as a teaching moment. He picks up the pieces and gives us another chance. We always have a choice in this life. Nothing goes against our free will. God always gives us the opportunity to hear Him. It is up to us to get in our secret place and open our ears and hearts to hear what He has to say.

Let me give you an example. Years ago, I had an incredible ministry opportunity come my way. I heard the loud knock at the door, and it was music to my soul. It was an incredible opportunity! Before opening that door, I turned to the Lord and asked Him what I should do. I fully trusted in Him and His timing for opportunities that arose in my life. I believed in "His" plan for me, not "my" plan for me. So I listened to Him, and He told me that it was not the right opportunity at the time. I can honestly say that I was a little disappointed, but I decided to listen and trust in Him completely.

I didn't understand it at that time in my life, but looking back, if I had decided to open that door and walk through, my life would have gone in a completely different direction than His plan. It probably

CHAPTER 5: UNFINISHED BUSINESS

would have been a disaster. Looking back, I'm confident that I made the right choice by not opening the door, even though it looked great. I might not be where I am today if I had made that decision without Him. God sees and knows all. He would have redirected me if I hadn't made the right choice and listened to Him. He would have given me other opportunities to close the door and get out. The question is: would I have listened?

God loves us so much and wants to see us walk in the fullness of what He has for each of us. Of course, He wants us to succeed! We are His children. Like any parent, we want our children to be successful, and we will do anything we can to help them along the way. When they make a bad decision or choice, we don't abandon them and say, "Oh well, you're on your own now!" or "You didn't listen to me! I told you so!" No, He is our loving Daddy who will try to set us back on the right path to our destiny.

Is there a cost to opening our own doors? Absolutely! It may take us longer to get where we need to go, and we may have to go through more tests and trials along the way. No one wants to keep going around the mountain. Our goal is to make it to the Promised Land. I can confess that I have opened up a few doors that were not meant to be opened. There were red flags along the way that I chose to ignore. God doesn't leave us to venture out on our own. He is speaking to us. He will warn us about doors that shouldn't be opened. Have you ever had a "bad feeling" about something? Go to the Lord. Seek Him, and you will find your answer.

There will be doors that come knocking ahead of schedule. Be aware that the enemy will do everything in his power to get you off track. His job is to get you off your path to destiny because he doesn't want to see you succeed.

Doors that are meant to be opened will open in God's timing. We are on His time, not ours. Trust in the Almighty and heed the passionate cry of our beloved. Take time to hear the gentle knock of the Holy Spirit. When you do, I promise that nothing compares to what's waiting for you on the other side.

> Furthermore, when I came to Troas to *preach* Christ's gospel, and a door was opened to me by the Lord. (2 Corinthians 2:12)

Let God be your bellhop and open the doors. You will feel important and loved beyond anything you could ever imagine! The carpet will be rolled out, and the trumpets will sound because the King of glory is announcing YOU! He will open the doors that should be opened to help guide you along your journey into the destiny God has waiting for you. What about your baggage, you ask? Leave it at the door. God wants you to leave your baggage behind. Not only does the Lord want to open our doors for us, He wants to carry our baggage. As we walk through the doors He has for us, He will carry our burdens so we will be able to set our eyes upon Him and the glory before us.

Baggage Claim Ahead

We all walk around with some type of baggage or burdens at some point in our lifetime; it's part of life. Lugging baggage around is stressful—both naturally and spiritually. God is ready and waiting to claim your baggage. Psalm 55:22 tells us to "Cast your burden on the Lord, and He will sustain you." God will provide us with what we need to let go of the things that are holding us back. Letting go is hard sometimes.

Look at it this way—if you saw your child holding onto something dangerous that would harm them, you would want them to drop or give it up so they wouldn't get hurt. That's how God sees our burdens. He knows they are harmful and He wants us to give them to Him. We are His children. If we are holding onto something that would potentially wreak havoc on our lives, of course, He wants us to give it up so He can handle it. God's got our back!

Our world is full of rules and regulations. Competition is everywhere we look. We see it in marketing, sports, housing, and unfortunately, even in ministry. There's even competition amongst ourselves. People are trying to outdo each other or trying to be like someone else in some

Chapter 5: Unfinished Business

way, shape, or form. Most of us strive to be the best we can be. And it can get the best of us. And it's tiring!

This world's system has been created to keep us wanting more and more, making some people materialistic in character, looking for the greatest and latest best thing. Our society has created one big ball of chaos! If we're not careful, life can be very stressful. Yep! I said it! We've all experienced it. How many times have you heard, "I'm so stressed out! I can't take it anymore!" It's gotten the best of us no matter how careful we are. It's a fact of life. One thing is for sure—stress is bad for our bodies! Stress causes the most unhealthy mindsets, and it can even hurt or kill us.

> For to be carnally minded *is* death, but to be spiritually minded *is* life and peace. (Romans 8:6)

We develop stress because of things in our lives that we have a hard time coping with. How can that be? Why can't we deal with the simplest things sometimes? The answer may be found in something we may have never even thought of—it may be years, in fact, maybe even before we were born.

Maybe something lurking in your past has you trapped in a cycle. Perhaps you felt rejected when your first girlfriend or boyfriend broke up with you for another person. Or when you were young and witnessed your parents constantly fighting and eventually ending up in divorce, so you were torn between two homes. Or how about that child who loses a parent to death and they feel abandoned. I could go on and on. Everyone has things in the past. I know one thing for sure: it was never the Father's intention for anyone to go through these painful events.

Because of consequences of these unintentional situations or painful events, the enemy found a way in. It may have been through sin or iniquity in our bloodline from our parents or previous generations. It could have been something we ourselves did. Maybe it was an unwise decision or as a result of disobeying God. These unhealthy "events" cause a deep root to grow within us. Over time, these roots grow and lie in wait for something to "pop up" and cause havoc in our lives. This is where stress and coping mechanisms come in.

Over time, we learn to develop coping mechanisms to help us deal with the stress of unfortunate or painful events. Some coping mechanisms we develop are not good. The good news is that we can learn to develop good coping mechanisms in response to stressful situations that cause us to trigger a reaction. For example, if you are a person who is quick to anger (I became this person because I was angry that my parents divorced and left me with a broken home when I was a young child), recognize that you are becoming angry, and choose to take a timeout, walk away from the situation that has triggered the anger, take a breather, or try to find a possible solution before going back to the situation.

I can tell you from experience that I have dealt with anger issues for a long time. It took time in counseling (healing and deliverance) to learn how to deal or cope with the situation positively rather than screaming and yelling (like I used to do), which would hurt those I loved or cared about. I often regretted my words or actions.

You may react just the opposite and suppress your anger. Dealing with suppressed anger isn't good. It will only create a time bomb, and eventually, you will go off. Another example might be that little girl who was rejected by her boyfriend for another. She may not even realize that she feels that way because her parents wanted a boy instead of a girl when she was born. Thoughts and words go to us even in the womb. That is why we need to be careful with our words and actions. They can cause dire consequences for others without us even realizing it. That little girl may grow up not understanding why she never felt "good enough."

I want to remind you that our goal is to be like Jesus. What do you see in the mirror when you look at yourself? Are you happy with what you see? How do you cope with stressful situations? Are you reacting in love? How do you feel about yourself? What emotions or thoughts pop up? Do you see yourself the way Jesus sees you? We have an awesome heavenly Daddy who never meant for us to go through painful, hurtful

CHAPTER 5: UNFINISHED BUSINESS

situations. God's original intent was never for us to live broken or wounded. Unfortunately, sin entered our world when Adam and Eve fell. Jesus came and took care of it all when He died on the cross for our sins. He was there for us then, and He is there for us now if we choose to go to Him. He wants to help us and heal us.

It's Time to Clean Your Room!

We've all been there. We've made a mess of things, and now it's time to clean up. I will bet that when you were a kid playing in your room all day long that your parents came in and said, "Clean your room! It's a mess in here!" Sometimes we get so wrapped up in what we're doing that we don't see the mess we have to clean up. We have to face the music. We can't run and hide. No more denying it.

We are not perfect human beings. What? I'm not perfect? No, I hate to break it to you, but you are not perfect. God created us in such a unique way. From the time we are born to the time we die, we are on a journey called life. And in this life, we have a blueprint created especially for us. Not one blueprint is the same.

> **As we walk along in our journey, God shapes us and molds us through trust walks, faithfulness, trials, tribulations, and, just simply put— relationship with Him.**

As we walk along in our journey, God shapes us and molds us through trust walks, faithfulness, trials, tribulations, and, just simply put—relationship with Him. He is shaping our character and nature to be like Him and what He has called us to be. Our journey guides us into walking into His fullness. When we are complete and walking in the fullness He has for us, our destiny has been fulfilled. A destiny that hears, sees, and dreams for us. Wow! Imagine that! My destiny that was specifically designed for me (my blueprint) is hearing my cry, seeing the road ahead, and dreaming for me to answer the call the Lord has for me. I have my own cheerleader rooting me on! "Come on, Sal! Stay the course! I will pick you up when you fall! Keep moving forward! You got this! Keep your eyes on Me!"

You might be thinking, "That sounds easy enough, but what about the skeletons in my closet? How do I clean those up? My room is REALLY messy! It's going to take a dump truck to clean this mess up!" I've heard it all before, and I am here to say again that our God is so good! Once we decide to take a good look at ourselves and make the decision to want to clean the mess up, God is right there. It doesn't matter what day it is or what time. He's there. He's not expecting us to clean up on our own—it can't be done. We need Him. He will direct us on our journey with what we need to deal with first.

> He's not expecting us to clean up on our own—it can't be done. We need Him.

The Lord has done that for me. There was a time when my house was out of order, and I was really struggling. I was at a place in my life where I needed some guidance, and I was not handling things too well on my own. God is so good because when He hears our heartfelt cry, He will answer. It happened one day when I had a visitation by an angel. I had seen her in previous encounters, so she was familiar to me when I saw her. This particular angel looked feminine in nature, and there was a softness about her (this is what I saw).

In this experience, there was a list of directions and things to put in order (clean up) on the wall. It was like a "to do" list. The angel saw that I wanted to complete the directions on the list, so she began to help me. My wife was also there, but she didn't know it was an angel. I was eager to begin "cleaning up," so I started to grab a large bag that seemed too

Chapter 5: Unfinished Business

heavy for my wife to pick up. As I leaned over to grab the bag, the angel told me that my wife could pick it up. I knew immediately that this bag was intended for my wife to clean up, so I left it for her.

As I continued to clean up my own mess, I began to ask the angel some questions. I was curious about her relationship with Jesus, and she told me she always wants to be around Him. She loves being in relationship with Him and glorifying Him. I asked the angel how I would remember the answers to what I was experiencing, and she handed me a notebook with notes. I told her I didn't want it to end, and she smiled at me. Then the experience was over.

That day was eye-opening for me. I knew I needed to get some things in order in my life, but I didn't know where to start. After this experience, it became easy for me to see what needed to be cleaned up and in what order it needed to be done. It is important to note that the Lord showed me that my wife had some cleaning of her own to do. He showed me this so that I would have grace for my wife as she went through her own "cleaning." I wanted to pick up the bag, meaning I wanted to carry her burden, but that is not for me to carry. My wife had to allow the Lord to work within herself to get her own life in order.

When you clean a house, you can't clean everything all at once. You have to start somewhere, either the kitchen, living room, bedroom, or bathroom. And it takes time! I don't know about you, but my wife loves it when I help her clean the house because she doesn't have to do it alone. It's more efficient when we both clean the house. God isn't looking for you to clean your own house (your house is you) by yourself. It cannot be done. He sees the underlying dirt that needs deep cleansing. He sees things we don't want to deal with.

Remember those coping mechanisms? It's like taking the dirt and brushing it under the rug. Jesus doesn't want that for you. He wants to lift the rug and do a thorough cleaning. He sees your hurts, pain, and sadness that you're incapable of dealing with on your own. Oh, another thing. There is no blame game here. God does not condemn or put the blame on anyone. It doesn't matter what kind of unhealthy lifestyle you're leading. If you feel unworthy of His love, then you're wrong! He will pick up the broom and start cleaning your house because He loves you so much and wants to see your destiny fulfilled.

So now you've decided to say yes to God's call on your life. I promise you this: Once you make that decision, there *will* be opposition. You will hear the enemy whispering in your ear. You will hear that subtle knocking for the door to open to your old lifestyle. Satan will make everything look good and so much better, but he is a liar! He will start to tell you that you can't do it or you're not good enough. He will whisper in your ear that it won't be worth it because it will take too much time to change or it will be too difficult. The enemy is good at is bringing up your past. Don't listen! Keep your eyes on Jesus and His love for you. There is no compromising or submitting yourself to dealing with the unfinished business you have in your life.

> Therefore submit to God. Resist the devil and he will flee
> from you. (James 4:7)

You must do your part and learn to submit yourself totally to God. It is a free will choice and God will never violate your free will. Things may get difficult, but you can do it. You can finish what was started. This unfinished business that you deal with in your life will give you new grace to finish the race. Isn't that great news! You can finish the race!

You've got your running shoes on and you're headed to the finish line. One thing I can tell you is that consistency is important. If you were running a race to finish, you wouldn't stop to walk the rest of the way and expect to finish as the winner. Consistency is key to anything we do in life. I can tell you from experience that it takes time to develop this pattern. First of all, you have to want it. Let's say you gained a few pounds and want to lose them. In order for you to lose weight, you have to be consistent in your patterns. You would have to be consistent in your eating and exercise patterns. I've been there and done that. I've fallen off the wagon, and who doesn't when your wife makes a homemade chocolate cake when she knows you're on a diet!

Chapter 5: Unfinished Business

Yes, we will stumble and fall. That's expected for us to grow and reach maturity. But when you fall, dust yourself off and get back in the race! Speak life over yourself. Make declarations. Say, "I am loved! I am awesome! I can do this! I am a child of God! He loves me!" Declare, declare, declare!

> Yes, we will stumble and fall. That's expected for us to grow and reach maturity. But when you fall, dust yourself off and get back in the race!

The Doctor Is in the House

We all go to the doctor for one reason or another; most of the time, it's just for a routine check-up to make sure we are healthy. Even if we feel healthy, we would want to know if there was some underlying health issue that we weren't aware of. It is like that for us spiritually. If there was some underlying spiritual issue, we would want God to reveal or diagnose the issue so we wouldn't hurt ourselves or mislead others. It's important to stay on course and keep ourselves in check so we don't go down a dangerous road. He is our doctor and healer. The Lord is always on call and will take us in whenever we need Him.

In order for us to stay on our A-game, sometimes we need serious counsel from the Giver Himself. Personally, sometimes I have to go into my secret place and ask the Lord to help keep me on track. This is when He may reveal things to me. It may be healing, repentance of sin or He may see that I have an unhealthy mindset that needs to be renewed. Whatever He may reveal, let Him do the work.

The key point in all this is that we do not become sin conscious—always thinking we are doing something wrong or are in sin. I don't walk around sin conscious, and it's harmful to anyone to do so. Even though we are looking within ourselves to diagnose a problem or issue, we should never rely on our own thinking or diagnose our own problem. Always ask Him to reveal what He wants you to deal with. When we are too busy looking at ourselves—either condemning ourselves or trying to be perfect—we are putting our focus on ourselves and not on our Father. When we humble ourselves before the Lord, we are asking Him to search us out and reveal things to us that can be hindering us from walking into our destiny.

Of course, we will make mistakes along the way, and there will be learning curves as we begin to walk in our calling. God knows that. He will use circumstances to test us and give us situations we can learn to use and steward what He has given us. This is when we need to be aware of His voice so we can be obedient to Him and not be overcome with pride that we only are hearing ourselves. We need to make sure we are doing His will and not ours.

As believers, we always need to be on alert. Danger lies ahead. The enemy would love to see you fail and he will do everything to see you not fulfill the destiny God has for your life. This is why it's so important to stay close to the Lord. He is our protector. He defends us and helps guide us through these treacherous times. We can easily veer off course and get stranded. The enemy always makes things look good, but he is a counterfeiter.

> And no wonder! For Satan himself transforms himself into an angel of light. Therefore *it is* no great thing if his ministers also transform themselves into ministers of righteousness, whose end will be according to their works. (2 Corinthians 11:14-15)

He is a liar, a deceiver, and a cheater. He will do his best to try to trick us so we will fall. If we are not careful and allow our disorderly conduct, childish ways, or unfinished business to operate within us, "hooks" will allow an open door for the enemy to come in and get you off course. Even though he is not invited, he will barge his way in. We need to deal with pride, anger, busyness, selfishness, pain, unhealthy mindsets, or anything else that gets in our way of walking into the fullness. It's up to

Chapter 5: Unfinished Business

us to make sure we are cleaning ourselves up so to be the best we can be. We should be standing out among others because we are squeaky clean—not a speck or wrinkle on us. Looking into the mirror, we should see all that is good and holy. Our lives should reflect the life of a King.

Part 3: Life of the King

What would it be like to be a king? It sounds exciting, but let's be serious for a minute. Really think about it. What does it really mean to live the life of a king? Think of the responsibilities alone. Yikes! I imagine there is a lot of weight on the shoulders of kings. People are looking to you for answers, to feel safe and cared for, to be protected, governed, and the list goes on and on. And what about the character or virtues of a king? I know for sure there is only one king I would want to be like, and that is King Jesus. It is His patterned life that I choose to follow. His royal blood runs through my DNA that makes me a royal heir as His son. The intimacy I share with my King is how I learn to be like Him, to live like Him, and to love like Him. That's what He desires of us. Let the transformation begin!

Restored Inheritance

As the little prince grew, he was eager to train and learn the ways of a king. He followed his father's every footstep. The prince adored his father and grew in the likeness of him. When his father spoke, he listened intently to his words and began to teach others what he was learning.

The King's Bridal Company

The son recognized that his father stood for righteousness and wanted to follow in his ways.

As he became a young man, the prince learned to fight with a sword and planned strategies for battle. He could be as gentle as a flower and speak truth in love. The prince became strong and gained much wisdom over the years. The king knew the importance of the role his son would step into and the qualities needed to be a good king. The position of king came with authority and power. His son would learn how to steward the authority and power with perfect righteousness and honor.

The time had come for the prince to take possession of the kingdom. The king knew in his heart the ultimate sacrifice his son would have to make to be king. Life as he knew it would be over. He had to devote his body, soul, and spirit to the kingdom. This would be the greatest battle of his life. It was time to take back the kingdom.

The prince set off to reclaim what was rightfully his. With his trained army behind him, he led the way to conquer the darkness within the kingdom. The force of the prince and his mighty army was so powerful that the enemy fled. The battle had been won!

The kingdom was restored back to the perfect paradise it once was, and all things that were lost were now redeemed. The prince had saved the kingdom, and he was now ready to become king. In that exact moment, he knew what he was created for. He knew that his destiny was to fulfill the will of his father. The prince knew in his heart that he was born to reign over his father's kingdom. His time had come.

The sun shone brightly as the prince stood facing his father. He knelt before him, and the royal crown was placed upon his head. Cheers rose up as the prince was proclaimed king of kings. He stood, proudly facing his father. His father's love for him pierced his heart as he looked into his eyes. As the new king stood before his people,

Part 3: Life of the King

he was accepted and honored because he represented the character and nature of his father. He was a righteous king and reigned with love, grace, and mercy. The new king was now ready to find his bride.

Chapter 6: Supreme Royalty

Royal DNA

Most of us reading this book probably have never met anyone face-to-face who is of true royal descent. The closest we get to them is through social media and TV. They seem to stand out from everyone else. They walk and move with a confidence that is set apart from those around them. So what is it that causes this to happen? I believe it is the knowledge that they have royal blood flowing through their veins; royal DNA.

As a person of royalty, you know that you merely speak a word, and others around you will jump to fulfill it. There's no stress of how you will pay the bills or make ends meet—you have the wealth of the whole kingdom at your fingertips! There's no question as to who you are; you have royal DNA—and everyone around you knows it! People come from far and wide just to shake your hand or snap a selfie with you. Just being in your presence is exhilarating to others.

In the natural, there is a fine distinction that can be seen displayed in the life of someone who is of royal status. Likewise in the spiritual, there is also a fine distinction that can be seen in the life of someone who has accepted Jesus as their Lord and Savior *and* has learned to display His character and nature as sons and daughters of their true king—King Jesus.

The King's Bridal Company

Accepting Jesus washes us in the blood, and His blood starts to flow through our veins. Once we come to Jesus, He adopts us into His family. And His adoption is so complete that it's as though we had been born naturally into the royal family of God! We are truly His son or daughter, inheriting every right and privilege that comes with the territory. We should be walking with that royal confidence as we go about our lives.

So why do so many Christians think and act like the servant in the palace instead of taking on the likeness of the royalty that they have inherited? I believe it's because *they don't realize that they really are royalty!*

When Jesus told His disciples that they should serve one another and that those who wanted to be the greatest in the kingdom should become the least, He wasn't talking about giving up the royal status that we gained upon our salvation. He was trying to get our hearts and motivation to be in the right place so that we are doing everything on the basis of love for each other and not for personal gain. He never intended for us to lose our position of royalty in the kingdom.

> If you really know and understand your place in the kingdom as a son or daughter of the Royal King, you don't beg and plead; you speak with confidence and call things into being.

Why do so many people feel like they have to beg God just for their prayers to be heard and maybe possibly answered? Could it be that they have forgotten who they are? If you really know and understand your place in the kingdom as a son or daughter of the Royal King, you don't beg and plead; you speak with confidence and call things into being.

There is a time in the Bible when Jesus wanted to get figs off a fig tree and there weren't any. He cursed the fig tree, and it immediately shriveled up. The disciples were astounded by this, but look at Jesus' response to them:

> So Jesus answered and said to them, "Assuredly, I say to you, if you have faith and do not doubt, you will not only do what was done to the fig tree, but also if you say to this mountain, 'Be removed and be cast into the sea,' it will be done. And whatever things you ask in prayer, believing, you will receive." (Matthew 21:21-22)

Did you get that? Jesus said that whatever we ask for in prayer, if we will just believe, we will see it come to pass! How many times do we pray without really believing—deep in our heart—that it will happen? That's why we have to realize that we have royal DNA. It is a game-changer when it comes to walking out our Christian lives and our God-given purpose.

The Virtues of a King

When someone is royal, certain characteristics will mark their life. There is a quality that is different than the rest of the general population. As they grow in their knowledge of who they are as royalty, their life will reflect these attributes, some of it learned, and some because of their position.

Honor

Webster defines *honor* in several ways. A few of them are:

> Excellence of character; high moral worth; specifically in men, integrity; trustworthiness; in women, purity; chastity. A nice sense of what is right, just, and true, with corresponding course of life.[2]

---

2. Webster's Collegiate Dictionary, s.v., "honor," (G. & C. Merriam Co., Springfield, MA: 1913).

The King's Bridal Company

A royal person not only knows what is right, but they will also show it through their day-to-day lifestyle. It's not just something they talk about with empty words; they live it. Not only does their life demand honor and respect from others because of their position and status, but they will treat others with honor and respect as well because it flows out from them.

When you're around someone who doesn't have honor in their life, you probably won't want to be around them for very long. It affects every area of life, and it will repel others away from them. It's like a bad smell that just won't wash off—you don't want to be around it! As a child of the King, our lives should hold a sweet aroma of honor and respect that everyone around will want to experience.

There is one additional point I want to make here about honor. As sons and daughters of King Jesus, we need to learn to represent Him when it comes to honoring others. When we see others through the eyes of God, we are seeing them through His perspective. He sees their hurt, their pain, and knows what they have walked in. We cannot treat others by what we "see" or "hear" with our natural senses. When Jesus walked the earth, He honored all those He met. He honored the sick, the poor, the lost, the sinners, the righteous, and the faithful. He walked this earth as a servant and taught His disciples to do the same.

> So when He had washed their feet, taken His garments, and sat down again, He said to them, "Do you know what I have done to you? You call Me Teacher and Lord, and you say well, for *so* I am. If I then, *your* Lord and Teacher, have washed your feet, you also ought to wash one another's feet. For I have given you an example, that you should do as I have done to you. Most assuredly, I say to you, a servant is not greater than his master; nor is he who is sent greater than he who sent him. If you know these things, blessed are you if you do them. (John 13:12-17)

We need to learn to lead by example—His example. Learning how to honor people involves a deep look at your own identity. If you cannot

Chapter 6: Supreme Royalty

see that you are truly awesome and amazing through His eyes, then how can you possibly walk in the greatness and characteristics of royalty? Honor doesn't come automatically just because we are saved. Honor is a journey that comes from intimacy with our king. Honor also comes when we have a reverential fear of the Lord. When we become His humble servants, then we can truly understand that honor and greatness can only come from Him. When we learn to honor Him first, then we learn how to honor others with grace and through the eyes of love.

Excellence

As royalty, everything you do and touch should have a fine sheen of excellence on it. That's what will set you apart.

In the natural, if a king throws a grand ball or event, he doesn't just show up and expect things to happen. There's nothing that will be done halfway or just okay. There is detailed planning and preparation that will go into every part of it so that when all the guests show up, it's something that everyone will enjoy and talk about for days afterward. Their excellence in what they do sets them apart from the general population.

But excellence isn't just an attribute; it can be a whole way of life. It's the concept of leaving things better than the way you found it. It's going above and beyond when you don't have to. A lifestyle of excellence will stand out when others just do enough to get by.

Daniel had a spirit of excellence, and this is what helped thrust him into higher positions, even in the eyes of the king.

> Then this Daniel distinguished himself above the governors and satraps, because an excellent spirit *was* in him; and the king gave thought to setting him over the whole realm. (Daniel 6:3)

As children of God, we should naturally want to do everything in our lives to please God—and when we truly do that, we won't leave anything halfway done; we will complete it the best way that we can and with excellence. This is what Paul meant in Colossians 3:23 when he said, "And whatever you do, do it heartily, as to the Lord and not to men." You don't have to have a lot of money to have excellence in your life either; you just use what God has given you to the best extent that you can.

Dignity

Perhaps one of the most identifying features about someone who has royal DNA is that they walk, talk, move, and act with an air of dignity. This isn't to be confused with someone who is snobbish or self-absorbed, but it is that confidence displayed that causes others to look at them and wonder why they're so different.

Webster defines *dignity* as "a state of being worthy or honorable; elevation of mind or character."[3] And here is where we find the key to really showing dignity as a child of the King: worth.

Many Christians go throughout their lives with a sense of not being worthy. They look at their past and all of the mistakes they've made, and they resign themselves to just not being acceptable. They look at their weaknesses and sins that they easily fall into, and they don't feel as though God can really keep forgiving them over and over when they will inevitably screw up again. They see their own shortcomings and wonder why God would ever want to use them for His purposes.

If that describes any way that you are feeling, take a good look at these scriptures below that declare your worth to God and His kingdom:

> Each time he said, "My grace is all you need. My power works best in weakness." So now I am glad to boast about my weaknesses, so that the power of Christ can work through me. That's why I take pleasure in my weaknesses, and in the insults, hardships, persecutions, and troubles that I suffer for Christ. For when I am weak, then I am strong. (2 Corinthians 12:9-10 NLT)

---

3. Webster's Collegiate Dictionary, s.v., "dignity," (G. & C. Merriam Co., Springfield, MA: 1913).

Chapter 6: Supreme Royalty

> For we are God's masterpiece. He has created us anew in Christ Jesus, so we can do the good things he planned for us long ago. (Ephesians 2:10 NLT)

> You are a chosen people. You are royal priests, a holy nation, God's very own possession. As a result, you can show others the goodness of God, for he called you out of the darkness into his wonderful light. (1 Peter 2:9 NLT)

We can walk with confidence and dignity, knowing that no matter what's in our past, present, or future, we are worthy and accepted by God and that He will use it all for His glory as long as we are submitted to Him and His plan and purpose for our lives. So let's lift up our heads, knowing that we have the full authority and backing of the kingdom of God on our side to help us through our everyday lives.

> **Let's lift up our heads, knowing that we have the full authority and backing of the kingdom of God on our side to help us through our everyday lives.**

Reverence

Reverence may not seem to be an attribute to some people, but it is another state of being that is reflected in the life of a king. *Reverence* means "profound respect and esteem mingled with fear and affection."[4]

We can easily see how reverence is shown to those in high-up positions, and also to our Lord, But this is also a characteristic of who we are as royalty. I also believe that reverence is reciprocal—it can be both given and given back. When you show reverence toward someone,

---

4. Webster's Collegiate Dictionary, s.v., "reverence," (G. & C. Merriam Co., Springfield, MA: 1913).

it will produce a similar reaction—and they will show that same respect and esteem back to you.

As we grow into our position of royalty, we will naturally begin to show more reverence toward God and toward the people around us. It's just one more qualifying evidence that we truly are being conformed to our identity as sons and daughters of the King and that we are accepting our status as royalty.

Showing Our Fruit

When we start to walk in these royal virtues, we also take on other attributes as well, living virtuously as kings and, by nature, exuding the fruit of the Spirit through our lives. Paul tells us very clearly what this will look like in the book of Galatians:

> But the fruit of the Spirit is love, joy, peace, longsuffering, kindness, goodness, faithfulness, gentleness, self-control. (Galatians 5:23-24)

I want to talk about just a few of these "fruits" that should be very evident in the life of a child of the King.

Love

Love is the greatest display of God's character in our lives. We can do all kinds of things "for the kingdom," but if our ultimate motivation for doing it is not based on love, it's all for nothing and will fall to the ground, completely unfruitful.

> Though I speak with the tongues of men and of angels, but have not love, I have become sounding brass or a clanging cymbal. And though I have *the gift of* prophecy, and understand all mysteries and all knowledge, and though I have all faith, so that I could remove mountains, but have not love, I am nothing. And though I bestow all my goods to

Chapter 6: Supreme Royalty

feed *the poor,* and though I give my body to be burned, but have not love, it profits me nothing. (1 Corinthians 13:1-3)

Paul explains it above in what we all know as the "love" chapter of first Corinthians 13. But this chapter doesn't speak very much about romantic love, as everyone seems to think; what really hit the nail on the head is having love—love for God and love for others—as the backbone for everything we do!

The bottom line is that you need to take a good long look at your actions and the reasons behind why you do the things you do. Is it out of love, or is it to be seen and to get noticed? Do you do something good just so you can post a selfie on social media as soon as possible so everyone can leave a comment about what a wonderful thing you did, or do you do it because you love God and people so much that you can't help yourself, and do it secretly so God can reward you?

Joy

I have been in social gatherings with other believers where I thought maybe a funeral just happened. It's sad but true! If there's one thing the enemy wants to do, it's to steal your joy.

How many times do you go to church, and it seems like everyone you talk to just had a bowl of lemons for breakfast before they came to church? They are so consumed with this problem and that issue that they allowed the enemy to steal away the joy from under them, leaving them a sour-faced mess!

It's easy to get caught up in our issues and problems, and instead of praying about those things and leaving them at the feet of Jesus, we pick them right back up, throw them over our shoulder like a heavy backpack that we feel we have to carry, dragging it around with us. Not only that, but when others share their problems with us, instead of offering to pray right then and there about it and getting joy and victory over it, we sling THEIR problems across our back—adding to the already-heavy weight that we are carrying! It's no wonder believers deal with depression sometimes just as often as unbelievers—you weren't designed to carry those heavy burdens. Jesus Himself said that He wants to carry them for us.

> Come to Me, all *you* who labor and are heavy laden, and I will give you rest. Take My yoke upon you and learn from Me, for I am gentle and lowly in heart, and you will find rest for your souls. For My yoke *is* easy and My burden is light. (Matt. 11:28-30)

Peace

If there is one fruit of the spirit that often gets overlooked, I believe it is peace. Especially in the day and age we live in. Everyone is so filled with fear and uncertainty about the future. World events, sicknesses, violent outbreaks, worldwide pandemics have swept across the world—not just our country—the entire planet! If ever there was a time when it seems to be okay to be afraid, it would be right now.

In Jesus' final days before He faced death on the cross, some of His final and most powerful words that He left with His disciples was to not be afraid but to be filled with peace.

> Peace I leave with you, My peace I give to you; not as the world gives do I give to you. Let not your heart be troubled, neither let it be afraid. (John 14:27)

One major earmark of the King's children is that when everything has been turned into a huge chaotic mess, they are full of peace and light, keeping their eyes focused on the Lord and their mission—not being swayed by the tumult around them.

One of the biggest battles we face today is overcoming the fear that media, politics, and the enemy strives to implant into our minds. We have to constantly remind ourselves that God is in control and seek peace in our hearts. This way, we can make rational, god-filled judgments and decisions about the future and the world around us so that we can be the salt and light that Jesus intended for us to be.

Chapter 6: Supreme Royalty

The Beatitudes

In the famous message that Jesus spoke on the hilltop called the Sermon on the Mount, Jesus gave us a whole list of people who are blessed in certain situations, called the Beatitudes. I believe that taking on the heart-position of these Beatitudes is critical for progression in becoming true sons and daughters of the King.

Let's take a look at these Beatitudes:

> Blessed *are* the poor in spirit, for theirs is the kingdom of heaven. Blessed *are* those who mourn, for they shall be comforted. Blessed *are* the meek, for they shall inherit the earth. Blessed *are* those who hunger and thirst for righteousness, for they shall be filled. Blessed *are* the merciful, for they shall obtain mercy. Blessed *are* the pure in heart, for they shall see God. Blessed *are* the peacemakers, for they shall be called sons of God. Blessed *are* those who are persecuted for righteousness' sake, for theirs is the kingdom of heaven. (Matthew 5:3-10)

Most of you reading this could probably have quoted those from memory rather than read them, but have you really put the core values of each of those into practice? This is the key!

I don't have the time or space in this book to go deeply into each of these. There's so much "meat" packed in those seven verses! But let me expound a bit on a few of them, and you will see how they connect with the fruit of the Spirit.

Blessed Are the Poor in Spirit

> Blessed *are* the poor in spirit, for theirs is the kingdom of heaven. (Matthew 5:3)

What does it really mean to be "poor in spirit"? It's not about acting spiritually impoverished, having the position of cowering around the

Lord, or having to beg and plead with God for things. It's more about the realization that we are spiritually bankrupt without Him—the discovery that nothing and nobody can help us get rid of the sin in our lives except our amazing God.

Being poor in spirit reflects a desperation toward God that results from knowing we need Him in every area of life and that apart from Him, we can do nothing. This is what Jesus was trying to get across to His disciples when he was talking with them before He was crucified:

> Remain in me, and I will remain in you. For a branch cannot produce fruit if it is severed from the vine, and you cannot be fruitful unless you remain in me. Yes, I am the vine; you are the branches. Those who remain in me, and I in them, will produce much fruit. For apart from me you can do nothing. (John 15:4-5 NLT)

Out of this position of desperation will flow a deep desire to keep Jesus in the very center of everything we do.

Blessed Are the Meek

> Blessed *are* the meek, for they shall inherit the earth (Matthew 5:5).

The world may look at those who are meek as people who are quiet, won't argue, and who become a doormat, just following along with the crowd, but this isn't the image that Jesus was trying to convey with the word *meek*. Being meek is to be completely humble and gentle, not only toward other people but also toward God. It involves accepting that what God allows in your life is for a reason and is for good.

The life of Jesus models this humility. We know that He was completely human as well as being completely God. In His humanity, He could have chosen whatever He wanted to do, but He accepted that God's plan for His life was to die on the cross. Here is how Paul describes this:

Chapter 6: Supreme Royalty

> Who, being in the form of God, did not consider it robbery to be equal with God, but made Himself of no reputation, taking the form of a bondservant, *and* coming in the likeness of men. And being found in appearance as a man, He humbled Himself and became obedient to *the point of* death, even the death of the cross. (Philippians 2:6-8)

Jesus lived his life in a way that we are supposed to be able to model our walk with God after. Because He walked out meekness and humility, we can do it too. Because He was totally submitted to whatever Father God had for Him to do, we can have the same attitude and perspective in our lives. Some people may not be asked to die for their beliefs like Jesus did, but we should always be ready to if we are faced with that situation.

Blessed Are the Pure in Heart

> Blessed *are* the pure in heart, for they shall see God. (Matthew 5:8)

The believer who is pure in heart is completely sold out for the Lord. There will be no hidden motives or hypocrisy found within them at all. The reason it says that those who have gotten to this place of being pure in heart will be able to see God is because they will be so transparent that His reflection and likeness will be mirrored in their lives—and others around will be able to easily see Jesus through them.

The pure in heart will have a desire to please God in every area of their life. They will be marked by not wanting to compromise their faith or beliefs for any reason. Being pure in heart and holiness go hand-in-hand, as we see in Hebrews 12:14 (NLT):

> Work at living in peace with everyone, and work at living a holy life, for those who are not holy will not see the Lord.

When we truly begin to walk in the Beatitudes and implement what Jesus was saying through them, we will start to be more than conquerors and will be able to see true victory in our lives. When we put them into practice, we will naturally develop godly character that will set us apart and give us a solid understanding of what it is to be royalty from God's perspective.

Then a phenomenon will take place as we apply the truths of the Beatitudes along with having the fruit of the Spirit evident in our lives. When we truly learn these things, we learn what our identity is as a royal, and then we can truly know where we come from as sons and daughters. As we walk all these attributes out, we will begin to act and think like a true king. It is what will help us distinguish between earthly royalty and kingdom royalty.

Supreme Believers

When we take those virtues of the king that we talked about earlier in this chapter and combine them with the Beatitudes and the fruit of the Spirit, I believe that this is where believers really become "supreme." This isn't supreme in the sense that we are as great as God, because Jesus told us plainly that kingdom greatness is very different from how the world sees greatness.

> Kingdom greatness and supremacy are all about being able to emulate Jesus' example of going low and becoming a servant.

In Mark 9:35, Jesus told His disciples, "If anyone desires to be first, he shall be last of all and servant of all." Kingdom greatness and supremacy are all about being able to emulate Jesus' example of going low and becoming a servant. Unfortunately, this is not how we are taught

Chapter 6: Supreme Royalty

to operate in many churches today. They may talk about how the last shall be first, and the first shall be last, but if you really look at how they are training people to operate in ministry, they've got it all backward!

Putting the Cart before the Horse

There are whole bodies and systems of churches where a large emphasis is placed on finding people's giftings and offices and on healings, miracles, and other supernatural things. Now, don't get me wrong, these are all great in the body of Christ; however, the main emphasis should not be solely on the gifts within us, but also the essence of who we are and WHO we represent. I'm talking about the substance (our character and nature) within us.

Places like this will do a lot of training about spiritual gifts and how to operate in them, but they put so much weight on equipping people in these areas that they ignore any substantial training about having godly character and the nature of God. They forget to teach on what's important through the process. It seems like they put the cart before the horse, when in reality, godly character and nature should be established along with finding out who we are and what we are called to do.

God allows us to function in our gifts so He can get our attention. Our gifts are supposed to draw us to King Jesus; if not, then something is out of order in our own personal lives. Without having the essence of Jesus to sustain what God has given us, we most likely will get carried away putting the emphasis on ourselves rather than Him. Unfortunately, the enemy can come in and destroy what God is trying to do through us.

There needs to be a progression of training for those who want to step into what God has called them to do. Jesus' disciples were called and taught by Jesus Himself for three years before they were released into ministry. As they were learning about healings, miracles, and other supernatural events, they were also learning about Jesus' character and nature and what it meant to walk in the kingdom. He equipped them, trained them, and released them. We need to be like the disciples, watching and learning at the feet of someone who has been down the road and represents the character and nature of Jesus.

THE KING'S BRIDAL COMPANY

Paul tells us how we should be walking out our call in the book of Ephesians:

> I, therefore, the prisoner of the Lord, beseech you to walk worthy of the calling with which you were called, with all lowliness and gentleness, with longsuffering, bearing with one another in love. (Ephesians 4:1-2)

Once we have the knowledge that we can be supreme royalty in the sense of going low like Jesus did, being humble and meek, completely submitted to the will of God for our lives, then we can move forward into stepping into our role as a son or daughter of the King and discovering the inheritance that has been laid up for us.

Chapter 7: Kingdom Inheritance

We've all seen a movie where at some point, the main character—who is typically down and out or just run-of-the-mill—suddenly discovers that they either have some type of royal bloodline or that they have a great inheritance that they had no clue about. It's fun to dream, right? That's why Hollywood has come up with so many similar storylines like that. But what if you were to find out that you *really do* have an inheritance coming that you didn't know about?

Noah Webster defined the word *inheritance* as "a permanent or valuable possession or blessing, especially one received without purchase; an estate received by descent as heir to another, or which may be transmitted to an heir."

Position versus Possession

There's a difference between what we receive from God upon salvation and the inheritance He gives us when He deems us ready to step into it. These are two separate truths that can get confusing if someone has not been taught the difference between them. I like to refer to these as positional truth and possessional truth.

Positional Truth

The moment when a person accepts Jesus into their heart as their Lord and Savior, they become a son or daughter of God. This truth has been communicated many times in Scripture. Here's just one:

> But as many as received Him, to them He gave the right to become children of God, to those who believe in His name. (John 1:12)

Positional truth says that we become sons and daughters when we come to know Jesus. Just like naturally born children, they don't have to do a single thing to have the title of son or daughter; the minute they are conceived, they are the child of their parents. Spiritually, when you come to Jesus, your position as a child of God is secured—but it is another thing to learn how to walk in that mantle of sonship.

Possessional Truth

In the natural, when someone is in line to inherit something, there is normally a process for when or how it will be passed on or obtained. There may be a certain age or level of maturity that must be reached in order for the person giving the inheritance to feel assured that the one on the receiving end will know how to use or manage that type of blessing, treasure, or wealth. It never changes the fact that the inheritance is due to them; it's already theirs by way of their position. They just need to be ready to receive it properly. This is what Paul is talking about in Galatians 4:1-2:

> Now I say *that* the heir, as long as he is a child, does not differ at all from a slave, though he is master of all, but is under guardians and stewards until the time appointed by the father.

The natural child has to be prepared to accept the inheritance. And until the father thinks that the child is mature enough, they do not get to receive the inheritance to manage and control. Spiritually, we have

Chapter 7: Kingdom Inheritance

to be prepared to come into our sonship in Christ, as Paul explains in Galatians 4:3-7:

> Even so we, when we were children, were in bondage under the elements of the world. But when the fullness of the time had come, God sent forth His Son, born of a woman, born under the law, to redeem those who were under the law, that we might receive the adoption as sons. And because you are sons, God has sent forth the Spirit of His Son into your hearts, crying out, "Abba, Father!" Therefore you are no longer a slave but a son, and if a son, then an heir of God through Christ.

As we go through this process and step into maturity as an heir, our identity starts to shift and our relationship with the Father changes. We see Him as Daddy, and not just as Creator and Judge as we did in our more immature stages. This marks a very crucial shift. Knowing God as Daddy leads us into greater measures of intimacy, and in turn, intimacy causes us to have a deeper desire to be conformed into the image of His Son.

"I'm Going to Steal Your Inheritance!"

Before I understood the importance of this truth about our inheritance, I had an encounter that shook me to the core and shifted my focus.

During prayer one day, I had an experience, and I was taken up out of my room and into the presence of what I initially thought was an angel that was stunningly beautiful. What shocked me was what came out of the mouth of this spiritual being.

As I was looking at it, it said, "The government is going to steal your inheritance."

I was taken back and just stared back at it and replied, "No, you're not!"

In response, it said, "Yes, we are. We are going to steal your inheritance. " Then the "angel" began to transform into a terrifying demonic being. It was very scary and took me by surprise.

All I could do was begin to plead the blood of Jesus. Suddenly I found myself back in my room.

During this time in my life, I was at a crossroads in many areas: business, family, etc. Everything that was an inheritance in my life was in jeopardy. Before this encounter, even though I understood what sonship was and that I had an inheritance, I had become complacent about it. I had the outlook that it was all fine and that I didn't need to fight really hard spiritually for my inheritance. I didn't realize the magnitude of the spiritual warfare that was going on around me and what was at stake.

After telling us about the armor of God, Paul gives us a very crucial instruction about prayer and how important it is for us to keep watch and persevere in prayer:

> Praying always with all prayer and supplication in the Spirit, being watchful to this end with all perseverance and supplication for all the saints. (Ephesians 6:18)

After having the encounter, my spirit was awakened to the warfare going on around me and that the enemy was trying to not only take away my inheritance but that my destiny was at stake too. It wasn't long before I got back on track and started taking possession over these areas in the spirit.

The enemy is out there trying to find any way possible to steal our inheritance from us.

We have to be aware that the enemy is out to steal our inheritance from us. I thank God that I had that encounter—as scary as it was—

CHAPTER 7: KINGDOM INHERITANCE

because it shook me up enough to be aware of all that the enemy was trying to do against me, my family, my business, and my future destiny—everything was at stake!

My friends, we have to realize that the enemy is out there trying to find any way possible to steal our inheritance from us. The only way to safeguard from this happening to us is to realize our true identity as a child of God and that we have the authority to take back control over those areas where the devil is trying to get a foothold. There is a progression to this.

The Making of a Son and Daughter

So what does a true son or daughter of God look like? What I have discovered is that there are certain characteristics that they will display. These may manifest differently from person to person, but the basic characteristic will be the same.

Always Growing

> So let us stop going over the basic teachings about Christ again and again. Let us go on instead and become mature in our understanding. Surely we don't need to start again with the fundamental importance of repenting from evil deeds and placing our faith in God. (Hebrews 6:1 NLT)

When someone begins to really embrace their position as a true child of God and chase greatness, they will always pursue maturity. They realize there is a growth process and will not be satisfied with staying where they are mentally, emotionally, spiritually, and often in many other ways.

Sometimes I meet people who come across as having already "arrived." They've been there and done that, and they believe they are at the peak of where they can be and that there's nothing more for them to learn. This type of thinking is a trap from the enemy and causes us to become complacent and stagnant in life.

We have to always remember that there is a process—and that we will always be in process! There's really no end to becoming mature; there are greater heights and deeper depths that we can dive into. Never stop growing!

The kingdom of God was never intended for people to live in alone. In fact, those who have received and embrace their position as a son or daughter will seek out people who are wiser and more established to become their spiritual mentor or spiritual father or mother. They will have no problem at all with accepting constructive criticism from these people who speak into their lives.

> Fools think their own way is right, but the wise listen to others. (Proverbs 12:15 NLT)

As we grow and mature, there comes a time when we are going to need help. We were never expected to try to do things on our own. The Lord wants us to always be dependent upon Him and not to become self-reliant. We have to understand that we are called to a corporate body, and within this body of believers, we all have a unique expression that, when used correctly, can help others walk into their God-ordained destiny. Before this can happen, we must learn to be accountable and teachable. We must be willing to be fathered or mothered just like a child. Whether you call it mentorship or fathering or mothering, it does not matter. What matters is that you are willing to humble yourself and say, "Wow! Maybe I just can't do this on my own." Ask the Lord to bring the right person or people into your life to help you grow up into the fullness you are created to be.

Ephesians 4:15-16 says,

> But, speaking the truth in love, may grow up in all things into Him who is the head—Christ—from whom the whole body, joined and knit together by what every joint

Chapter 7: Kingdom Inheritance

supplies, according to the effective working by which every part does its share, causes growth of the body for the edifying of itself in love.

These verses speak of growing up in all things. How can we grow and walk where we are called to without learning from the ones who have already walked there before? They have already gotten their feet wet. They have already paved the path. When I need help, I call for help. The people the Lord has sent into my life have taken me beyond what I could have ever achieved on my own in my lifetime. Mentors and spiritual fathers or mothers will be instrumental in the process of gathering the corporate bride together.

Become Teachable

You will say, "How I hated discipline! If only I had not ignored all the warnings! Oh, why didn't I listen to my teachers? Why didn't I pay attention to my instructors?" (Proverbs 5:12-13 NLT)

Someone can want help and still not be teachable. They may realize that having a spiritual advisor is a good thing, but when that person tries to speak into something they see as a problem in their life, the unteachable person will give excuses for why they can't change or just discount the wisdom as something less than it is.

Have you ever had someone give you constructive criticism, and it irritated you? Maybe it was about an area that is very sensitive or that you felt as though you were excelling in. Sometimes it's hard to be teachable! But it is crucial to our growth and to become the true son or daughter that God wants us to be.

We have to stay teachable and let our hearts be pliable, not just in the hands of the Father, but to the wisdom and knowledge of others as well. Of course, we can't just follow anyone's advice but learn to sort it out and find the true knowledge coming from a heart of love that is intended to help us ultimately grow and become a better version of ourselves.

When we hear these types of things and know that the motivation behind them is for our good, then we should take it into consideration. As I said before, God will place the right people in our lives to help us grow and mature in Him. God will use these people to speak His wisdom and revelation for our lives.

> We have to stay teachable and let our hearts be pliable, not just in the hands of the Father, but to the wisdom and knowledge of others as well.

Become Vulnerable

> I pray that your love will overflow more and more, and that you will keep on growing in knowledge and understanding. For I want you to understand what really matters, so that you may live pure and blameless lives until the day of Christ's return. (Philippians 1:9-10 NLT)

Paul shows us in the passage above that as we continue to grow and progress in our knowledge of God and in our position as a child of God, one thing that should naturally occur is that we should live pure and blameless lives, not having any hidden sins or things that hold us back from being all God wants us to be.

Those who are true sons and daughters are quick to confess their weaknesses to their spiritual mentors in order to stay in that vulnerable and transparent position. We need to have an understanding of how holding onto those things can jeopardize our calling and destiny. It's highly important for us to remain pure.

Chapter 7: Kingdom Inheritance

Learn How to Wait

> Wait patiently for the Lord. Be brave and courageous. Yes, wait patiently for the Lord. (Psalm 27:14 NLT)

> Be still in the presence of the Lord, and wait patiently for him to act. (Psalm 37:7 NLT)

One big earmark of the son or daughter of God is that they are no longer in a hurry—especially when it comes to prayer and spending time with the Lord. They are happy to sit and wait in His presence. Waiting on God isn't hard anymore; it's not a chore or something they do to check it off the list for that day. Spending time with God will become like a hobby to them, like second nature, because it's so familiar and desirable.

> One big earmark of the son or daughter of God is that they are no longer in a hurry—especially when it comes to prayer and spending time with the Lord.

There's also a difference in how they handle the times when God asks them to wait for an answer to prayer. No longer are they anxious, trying to take matters into their own hands, or even resorting to begging or pleading with God to respond. They realize that sometimes God just wants to do things on His own timeline—and things will turn out way better if they are patient and wait for Him to work it out.

Understand Accountability

The true child of God will understand accountability on two different levels. They will have a greater comprehension of how important it is to be both accountable to God and also to people.

Accountability to God

> Yes, each of us will give a personal account to God. (Romans 14:12 NLT)

It goes without saying that we will be accountable to God. Each one of us will stand before Him one day and have to answer for all the wrong things we did throughout our lives—as well as all the idle moments and thoughts that could have been used to build the kingdom and weren't.

But the fact that we are held accountable can't be the motivating factor behind why we want to do right in our lives. The reason should always be based on our love for Father God—we love Him, and that's why we want to steer clear of sin. He gives us the free will to choose to obey or not, and He is always pleased when we choose to obey out of our deep love and devotion to Him.

Accountability to Man

> As iron sharpens iron, so a friend sharpens a friend. (Proverbs 27:17 NLT)

> Two people are better off than one, for they can help each other succeed. If one person falls, the other can reach out and help. But someone who falls alone is in real trouble. Likewise, two people lying close together can keep each other warm. But how can one be warm alone? A person standing alone can be attacked and defeated, but two can stand back-to-back and conquer. Three are

Chapter 7: Kingdom Inheritance

even better, for a triple-braided cord is not easily broken. (Ecclesiastes 4:9-12)

It is very crucial for the child of God who is learning to step into their role as a son or daughter to understand how important interpersonal accountability is. As the passages above show, we really do need each other!

As I stated before, living and growing in the kingdom was never intended for us to do naturally on our own. It's hard enough with the enemy trying to come around and steal our inheritance and wreak havoc in our lives whenever possible, so having people around us who can help lift us up when we are struggling is very critical. Especially now in the days we are living in with all levels of crazy things that are going on! No matter what circumstances arise around us, we need to be there for one another.

Want to Serve Others

> For God is not unjust. He will not forget how hard you have worked for him and how you have shown your love to him by caring for other believers, as you still do. (Hebrews 6:10 NLT)

When we step into sonship, there will be a desire to bless the people around us, especially when we see someone with a need. This is how the kingdom of God is supposed to operate. Just like when the early church first started, and nobody lacked anything because they all gave each other what they needed, so it should still be today. Don't be surprised if you are led to help other people in a greater capacity than you experienced before; this is normal kingdom living!

Submissive and Honorable

> For the Lord's sake, submit to all human authority—whether the king as head of state, or the officials he has

appointed. For the king has sent them to punish those who do wrong and to honor those who do right. It is God's will that your honorable lives should silence those ignorant people who make foolish accusations against you. For you are free, yet you are God's slaves, so don't use your freedom as an excuse to do evil. Respect everyone, and love the family of believers. Fear God, and respect the king. (1 Peter 2:13-17 NLT)

When someone steps into their role as a son or daughter of God, the way that they respond to other people will change—sometimes drastically! This is true regarding those who are authority figures over their lives. The person who is submitted to God will reflect His heart in how they react and respond to human authority, even those they don't agree with or see eye-to-eye on issues that are important to them.

It is possible to show honor and respect toward a secular authority figure—even one who is doing or allowing things that you know go against Scripture and God's laws. The key is to keep your heart's posture innocent in God's eyes and not fall into the trap of saying or doing things that are disrespectful or dishonorable toward that person. It doesn't mean you agree with what they're doing; it means you are honoring God's Word by not becoming spiteful and spreading a bad attitude toward that person. It's the position you are respecting, not necessarily their beliefs, and you have to keep that in proper perspective.

This is such a hard area today—especially with social media. And especially when there are so many evils at work through government leaders who are trying to push an agenda that we know is not what God wants. It's easy to post things online and share other people's posts to get others to rally around your viewpoint, but we need to take a step back and ask ourselves what Jesus would be doing in that situation.

One of the best examples we have from Scripture of respecting authority is through the life of Joseph. If you read Genesis chapters 39-41, you will see that over and over, Joseph had reason more than most people to get upset about the way he was being treated by secular

CHAPTER 7: KINGDOM INHERITANCE

leaders over him. But over and over again, he kept his cool, followed God's guidance, and eventually—in spite of his being thrown in prison for things he didn't do—he was promoted by these secular leaders. I believe that it had a lot to do with his level of integrity, honor, and respect for those people who had done him so wrong.

How can we do this when, as humans, it may be hard to keep our emotions in check when we don't agree with those who have been put into positions of leadership over our lives? It's all about perspective. We have to always keep it in the forefront of our minds that we are not living and working and toiling to please these human leaders—we have to make sure we are doing everything for the glory of the Lord and for His pleasure over us. That will make all the difference!

This is what Paul was talking about when he was writing to the Colossian believers:

> Work willingly at whatever you do, as though you were working for the Lord rather than for people. Remember that the Lord will give you an inheritance as your reward, and that the Master you are serving is Christ. (Colossians 3:23-24 NLT)

Do you remember at the start of this chapter how we defined the word *inheritance*? It's a permanent or valuable treasure or blessing that is passed down to an heir. Here Paul reminds us that God will be giving us an inheritance as our reward for all the work that we do for the Lord.

Are you positioning yourself to serve Jesus when you go to your workplace, or are you just trying to please the human authorities over your job title? Maybe that dead-end position can turn into a promotion as you pour your heart into what you are doing, picturing Jesus as the one to reward you for your hard work, no matter what type of stuff you have to put up with during the process.

The King's Bridal Company

Spiritual Wealth and Treasures

When we are submitted to the Lord in everything we do, we set ourselves up to be on the receiving end of the spiritual wealth and treasures that God has for us.

When the word *treasure* is mentioned, there are many images that might come to mind. Someone might be picturing a big pile of gold, while someone else might be imagining rare and beautiful gemstones. Others may be thinking about their bank balance growing to an unimaginable number, and still others may envision material possessions such as a big house, fancy cars, or any number of desirable things they dream of owning. But these physical treasures can never compare to the spiritual treasures that God has for us.

So what are spiritual treasures? There are many places in the book of Proverbs where wisdom is said to be a treasure (see Prov. 3:13-15; 8:11). Jesus likened the kingdom of God to a treasure being found (see Matt. 13:44). Second Corinthians 4:7 says that we have God's light shining in our hearts, a great treasure hidden away in our earthly clay jar.

In truth, there are many aspects and qualities of our spiritual life in Christ that we can regard as valuable, but I don't want to spend a lot of time reviewing all of those—I want to talk about the greatest treasure of all that we experience as a son or daughter of God. And that is having HIM!

Jesus Himself is our great treasure and reward! For me, intimacy with the Father is the most rewarding experience and treasure in my life. And I have had a lot of different situations and experiences in my lifetime. I know what it is to have money to get things I want—and it's still worthless compared to having intimacy with the Father.

I know what it was like to live for the next thrill, the next thing that makes me happy. It was nothing compared to the excitement that comes from spending time in the presence of Jesus. I've lived with the comfort of knowing all my bills were paid and I had money to spare, and yet, intimacy with the Father is still way better than having security in earthly things.

Chapter 7: Kingdom Inheritance

Here's how Paul described it:

> Everything else is worthless when compared with the infinite value of knowing Christ Jesus my Lord. For his sake I have discarded everything else, counting it all as garbage, so that I could gain Christ. (Philippians 3:7-8 NLT)

As sons and daughters—heirs—we have an inheritance that is so exciting, it should give us the perspective to get up each day and live our lives with purpose and focus, not just trying to "get by" to the next day.

I challenge you to become the mature son or daughter of King Jesus and step into your royal role, claiming your spiritual inheritance. When you do, you will start to have supreme influence in many areas of your life.

Chapter 8: Supreme Influence

Most people have a goal of being able to influence others through their life in some way, shape, or form. Knowing that something you said or did had an impact on someone else for the better is a feeling like no other.

In today's society, there are so many people looking to individuals who are influencers in the realm of media, politics, and sports, but not everyone who is held in high esteem and standing in the glow of the limelight has gotten there the right way. And if they don't have a strong foundation, they are in danger of being toppled from their fragile tower.

Character Is Supreme

So many people try to fast-track their way to having influence. It's easy to want to take a shortcut and get there quickly, but what is often overlooked is that there is no shortcut to true influence. Those who get there by any other means than the way God intended for them to arrive in that position often don't have the ability to walk in it because they didn't take the time to prepare themselves for the responsibility and seriousness of it.

What I have discovered is that character has to be built into us to have the substance we need to walk in supreme authority. There is a process of walking in maturity that aids in the character-building process. And there is no shortcut for building character!

There are a few ways that people try to skirt around the character-building process. How is this possible? Because there are some things that will outshine character on the surface level, but these methods of gaining influence can easily fade or crumble without having the character and nature to back it up.

Gifting

People today flock to ministers and Christians who have "shiny" gifts. You know what I'm talking about. God may have gifted them with the ability to give very accurate prophetic words. Or maybe they lay hands on people, and most of the time, the people get healed. How about those who can sing the house down and the anointing of God comes in the room in power? Perhaps the person has the ability to teach complicated things and make them very simple and easy to understand.

It's easy for gifts to outshine character. What happens is that we see God moving through people in certain ways, and those people get elevated to a position of authority *mainly based on their gifting*. We think that everything else in their life must be in order because they are so used by God. Then when that unstable person falls, it injures the body because we never thought about the fact that maybe they weren't ready for that position of authority.

Titles

In my opinion, the Christian world today passes out titles far too easily. It seems we are always being introduced to another apostle, prophet, or bishop. And some of these titles are self-given. Why do we like having a title so much? Because it instantly gives us a step up in the eyes of those we are being introduced to—whether we earned that position or not.

There are people walking around with the title of "prophet" who were never given that position by God. Maybe they function with a gift of prophecy or just are used to giving a prophetic word here or there—but they don't have any right to claim the office of the prophet. People I know who truly walk in the office of the prophet don't even want to add the title to their name because they understand the weighty responsibility and seriousness of it!

> **In my opinion, the Christian world today passes out titles far too easily.**

What I noticed about the apostle Paul is that the more character was built into his life, the less he liked having titles. When he began his ministry, he was comparing himself to those people who were considered "superapostles," yet by the time he was close to death, he referred to himself as "the least of all the saints" or "the worst of sinners."

When you stamp a title on your name and don't go through the dealings of God that builds character into your life to actually operate in that position, you are setting yourself up for failure every time—my advice: avoid the title until God stamps it on you. And even when He does, you do not have to shout it out in the streets to everyone you meet.

Connections

Another area that can easily outshine character is the connections that people have with well-known celebrities, ministers, and ministries. Our world today wants everything fast—we don't want to stand in line or wait for anything to be ready for us. So it's easy to want to associate and affiliate ourselves with people who are already well-known, hoping that those connections will give us a leg up and a shortcut to what we are trying to accomplish.

This isn't always a bad thing, and there are times when God will give you those connections as a way to help you out. But the danger comes when you are not prepared for it, and you haven't had character built into your life first. And if you are looking to those connections to establish you more than you are looking to God, then those connections have become an idol—and God doesn't want any idols in your life!

There was a time in my life when I was connected to a very large ministry. It was so exciting for me and I really felt blessed. But then God showed me that I had begun to believe that those connections were going to establish me more than God could. Once I realized that, I took a step back so I could be established by God, not man.

I know of ministries that were basically handed all the connections and support they needed on a silver platter to get them going. This looks great and is a wonderful testimony, but they never went through the dealings of God to prove their character and that they were ready for it. Unfortunately, some of these ministers are lacking in Christlike character and are hurting people in their "rise to fame" in their world. This should never be!

Identity Is Supreme

We have already been talking about finding our identity as sons and daughters and realize who we are in the kingdom and our position. At this point, we have to begin to walk in our identity, not just realize it.

There is a phenomenon that can happen here when we begin to walk in authority and influence that we need to be careful of. In our desire to have influence, there can be a tendency to allow authority and influence to create our identity and dictate who we are. This is a faulty foundation and one that has to be reversed if you notice it starting to happen in your life.

There's a reason that I first talked about how character is supreme. This is because your identity needs to spring out of character. It has to come as a result of true growth in Jesus. Your relationship with the Father and the character that He builds into your life should be the thing that determines your identity, not the ministry position you hold or the gifting that you operate in, or any type of influence or authority you have. What happens if that position gets stripped away? Where would your identity be then?

CHAPTER 8: SUPREME INFLUENCE

Sometimes God will allow us to see that our identity was shaped through trauma, iniquity, fear, or so many other unintended things that were the result of the fall of man. When ministries or life, in general, are built on these negative attributes, then substance can never truly be built within us to sustain us through the storms of life. When a storm arises, we usually gravitate to the coping mechanisms that we created with the help of the enemy to try to withstand the storm. Because of this, we will try to depend on our ways and not God's. This results in a performance-based identity.

> **The dealings of God may be painful at times, but it's never done without purpose. He wants us to be the best we can be, and this process is what transforms our character.**

If we can learn to heed to the dealings of God—the molding, pruning, and refining within us—then we will learn to come to the end of ourselves. God will allow certain situations and circumstances that will disrupt our peaceful lives so that we can unearth all the "dirt and debris" within us. This helps us see that we are in the way (our flesh) of what He truly intends for us. The dealings of God may be painful at times, but it's never done without purpose. He wants us to be the best we can be, and this process is what transforms our character. Our identity needs to be conformed to that of His Son so we can withstand the winds of the storm.

> Therefore we do not lose heart. Even though our outward man is perishing, yet the inward *man* is being renewed day by day. For our light affliction, which is but for a moment, is working for us a far more exceeding *and* eternal weight of glory, while we do not look at the things which are seen, but at the things which are not seen. For

the things which are seen *are* temporary, but the things which are not seen *are* eternal. (2 Corinthians 4:16-18)

There was a season in my life when ministry was everything to me. It became my idol. It wasn't about furthering the kingdom or seeing a soul get saved, and it certainly wasn't about being conformed into the character of Jesus. Because of my pain and trauma, ministry was how I found affirmation. Once I realized that I had a gift and ability to communicate, my pain and trauma helped shape my identity into a performance-based identity. I watched as my friendships, family, and house fell out of order. I was going from place to place using my gift for myself rather than to glorify Jesus. I was insecure and seeking affirmation through people rather than looking to Him for my security. Through several dreams, the Lord showed me that I was performing for myself rather than for Him.

One dream was very specific about a basketball game where I was supposed to be a starter, but I was sitting on the bench. In the dream, I was wondering why I was benched. Over time, He began to reveal to me that I was being benched or taken out of the game so He could do a work in me. During this time, I began to go through healing for my pain and trauma. God allowed me to go through this season so I could see for myself that I needed healing for my brokenness. He wanted to make me whole. It was through this healing that my identity began to transform so He could use me for His purpose and not my own.

We have to be very careful to have our identity firmly rooted in the right place. That way, if the storm comes and blows away the titles and positions, we are still standing strong.

Relationship with the Father Is Supreme

This should go without saying, but it's an area that is so often overlooked and understated that it deserves some attention here. If our

Chapter 8: Supreme Influence

relationship with Father God is not where it needs to be, the authority and influence will not be coming from the right place.

Our relationship with the Father needs to be one full of intimacy and passion. There is a progression to how this relationship is built, and there are three different phases that we have to walk through to get to the right position.

Knowing of God

At this stage, we know about Him. We have been taught and trained about who He is and His character, but there is not an interpersonal relationship with Him. He still seems distant to us.

I would venture to say that many Christians sitting in pews at church merely know about God and don't have that personal relationship. They may have said a sinner's prayer years ago, but haven't dived deeper into that relationship.

Knowing God Personally

At this phase, we take the extra steps to start to build our relationship with God. Our life with God moves past just knowing about Him, and we have a relationship with Him. At this point, it's there, but not all that it could be. We have an active prayer life and most likely are at church every week, even serving and helping others, being used in our gifts. We let God into certain areas of our life and heart—but never move past this phase to the third, content to stay right here.

But I believe that this is mainly because people don't realize what's available to them in God. They have been taught and trained how to live in phase two and that this is how it is. That's why so many people camp out at this stage. They don't even realize the incredible love relationship that they could be having with the Father. They don't know the manifestations of His presence, experiences, and deep intimacy that they are missing out on!

Knowing God Intimately and Passionately

When you move on to the third phase, you dive deep into your relationship with God, not holding anything back. There are times when you may have other things to do, but you just can't wait to get alone with God again and hear what He has to say to you.

It's like when you first fall in love with someone and you just want to be around each other all the time; you can't wait to hear what they will say next. There will be times when you just listen—not going down a long list of prayer requests, as it's so easy to get in the rut of. These moments of listening and being quiet in His presence are when He will share heaven's secrets with you.

Out of this deep relationship is where our true authority and influence really springs forth. Knowing that Jesus really, truly lives inside of us is the catalyst that makes all the difference. It is His authority and influence working through us—not our own—that is influencing the others around us. Having this perspective is so crucial!

Only when we get to this final phase of our relationship with the Father will we be ready to operate in true authority. But we have to always realize that the end goal is not authority and influence—the end goal is Him! The authority and influence come naturally in the progression, but we have to always keep our eyes on Him—even after we have "arrived."

Stewarding Authority and Dominion

As we develop our love relationship with the Father, He will begin to grant us areas where we can have influence and dominion. But along with that comes times of testing because when He gives us an area to have dominion over, He will expect us to steward it. Once we have proven that we can handle that level of influence, He will be able to expand our territory even further. This continues as a cycle until God expands our authority to where He wants it to be.

Chapter 8: Supreme Influence

I want to talk about a distinction between this type of dominion and authority and what I am seeing in the church world today. When we talk about having dominion, many people think about ruling from the top, but the way Jesus teaches, your real heart needs to be wrapped up in ruling from the bottom.

> And He sat down, called the twelve, and said to them, "If anyone desires to be first, he shall be last of all and servant of all." (Mark 9:35)

It's not about being in the limelight and people seeing you on a platform that gives you influence and authority. It's about what you are doing behind the scenes—when nobody is around—that really matters the most! Even if your ministry is to be on the platform, it's what your life looks like when nobody is watching that is most important.

As we walk in dominion and authority, we have to always keep our love relationship with the Father as the center of what we are doing. We need the presence of God to fuel our influence. Dominion without presence is domination. It's not about being a ruler—it's about being a lover. It's all about helping people from the bottom and seeing them become all that God wants them to be.

> **Dominion without presence is domination. It's not about being a ruler—it's about being a lover.**

There's another thing that is happening in churches all over the world today that is very sad as well. There are people who have been tested and tried by God's dealings only to find themselves up against man's fleshly motives. Some people in high positions of authority will be used by the enemy to derail any plans of promotion God has planned for you.

This can be frustrating indeed when you have gone through the dealings of God and come out the other side—and yet man steps in the way and tries to keep you down out of their own insecurity or from some other fleshly motive. It's not that you are not willing to serve from the bottom; God knows that you are because you have been doing that all along! God will allow circumstances like this in our lives so He can see how we will react to certain situations that are sometimes the toughest to overcome. This is where we can be given the opportunity to show the true character that God is working in us. God is so good that He will work both sides of the situation to build Christlike character in all His children. Always remember that sometimes the toughest situations will bring us further promotion as long as we are walking in His authority and not ours!

Functioning from Heavenly Places

> But God, who is rich in mercy, because of His great love with which He loved us, even when we were dead in trespasses, made us alive together with Christ (by grace you have been saved), and raised *us* up together, and made *us* sit together in the heavenly *places* in Christ Jesus. (Ephesians 2:4-6)

There is a lot of talk going on in the day and age we live in about how we have influence and authority because we are seated in heavenly places in Christ. Although this is true, I want to point out that you really cannot get to that place of supreme authority that we have been talking about without going through the stages of becoming a son or daughter of God and going through the different stages of it—not just realizing your identity, but truly walking in it—this is where true influence that is pure and undefiled comes from. Our influence comes out of a divine revelation of Sonship.

Even though we have all of the inheritance of Christ and dominion handed to us when we enter into that covenant relationship with Christ,

Chapter 8: Supreme Influence

there is a process of learning how to handle authority and influence. You wouldn't put a newborn baby in the position of a king just because they hold the DNA for it, right? That child has to be groomed to be able to make the right decisions and rule the country with a level head and maturity. It's the same with us as heirs to the kingdom and children of the King—we have to be tested and tried to really be able to steward the influence and authority God wants to give us. It's already ours, but we may not be ready for it yet. And if we are not ready, it could actually hurt us in the long run if we try to step into it prematurely.

Once we go through the proper process and the Father deems us ready and able to handle the authority and position that he has for us, then we can start walking in it. What authority do you have if you haven't walked through the process? This is where many people end up cutting their time short—by not preparing themselves or waiting for the Father's timing.

I urge you today: be patient in the process. Learn how to enjoy the moments as you walk through the journey to having true influence. It will be that much sweeter when you arrive and are able to function in grace and mercy, knowing that others are in process too. You will be able to see people from a different perspective because you were there in the process at one point, and you will know what it took to get there.

Part 4: The Bridal Company

True love….it's what we all want in life. It's what we yearn for. But what is true love really? How do we know it's really love? When I met my wife and fell in love, I knew she was the one for me. The love was so pure, honest, and real that I knew in my heart there was no other who could make me feel the way she could. She was the only one for me. That is how I feel about Jesus. Nobody else can make me feel the way He does. I know it is true love! My entire being knows and feels His love for me. It is such an amazing feeling to know that someone loves me through all my pain, sorrows, faults, weaknesses, joys, happiness, strengths, and faithfulness. He loves me just the way I am. That is the greatest love of all!

The Greatest Love of All

Since she was a little girl, she dreamed of her wedding day. She had been groomed her whole life in hopes of one day being chosen by the king himself to become his wife. For most girls, this would be a dream. In her world, it was reality. She was part of a royal family. In her kingdom, the king's bride would have a royal bloodline. Her father and mother felt so blessed when their daughter was born. Their princess would grow and learn the ways of becoming a queen someday. As their daughter grew, they made sure she remained humble and righteous. They wanted their daughter to be represented by the true character and nature of who she really was—royalty.

Her parents knew the importance of representing royal qualities. They wanted her to realize she was blessed beyond measure, yet at the same time keeping her from becoming prideful because of who she was. She learned to love others unconditionally regardless of who they were or where they came from. The princess learned to serve others and to help those in need. She was graceful and merciful, always quick to forgive. She had a love about her that glowed from within. Her presence would bless those around her.

The time came when their little princess grew to the age to be sent to the king's palace in hopes of catching his eye. Many other princesses were also sent from other royal families, hoping their daughter would be the chosen one. But there was something special about the one princess who stood out far above the rest. Her beauty immediately captivated the king's eye. But something else drew him to her. He watched her closely as she interacted with those around her. He saw her true beauty. It was coming from within. The king watched as she humbly helped his servants serve the guests. She was not ashamed. Her smile filled the room with such love and radiance. At that moment, he knew he had found his bride.

He could wait no longer to let everyone know that a decision had been made. The king walked up behind the princess he had chosen to be his bride. He tapped her on the shoulder, and she turned around to be face-to-face with the king. The princess was awestruck! The king was looking at her with such love and

PART 4: THE BRIDAL COMPANY

adoration. As her eyes found his, her heart fluttered with excitement. She bowed her head slightly as he grabbed her hand and got down on one knee. The crowd became silent as they watched the princess and the king. He looked up at her and asked the question she had been waiting for her whole life. "Will you be mine forever?" he asked. She knew instantly that she loved the king with all her heart. She exuberantly said yes, and the crowd erupted in a loud cheer.

At that moment, she realized that her dream had come true. Yes, she was marrying a king, but not just any king. Her hopes in all the years of waiting and preparing were that she would find her greatest love. She didn't want to just marry a king; she wanted a lover—someone with whom she would share her most intimate moments. A lover who would care about her and not the things of this world: she finally found her first true love!

Exhilaration filled her as she thought about the life that lay ahead with the king. Yes, they will be surrounded by splendor and majesty, but the love, joy, and peace that would encompass her meant more to her than any earthly possession. She would feel safe and protected in his strong arms and knew that no matter what she said or did, he will always love her unconditionally. She couldn't wait for the day to arrive when she would be his.

Chapter 9: The Desperate Cry

The day the Lord found me in the woods stoned out of my mind was the day that changed my life forever. I had overdosed on drugs, and suddenly I wanted to live and not die. They say when you are about to die, you see your life flash in front of your eyes. Well, I can tell you that it's real! All my sins from my teens to that day played like a movie reel in my mind in an instant. I knew I was going to die. I cried out, "Jesus Christ, if You really are the Son of God, then please give me another chance!" In my desperation, He answered me. I suddenly started to feel my body going back to normal. That near-death experience altered my life forever. I desperately wanted Jesus. It was the day I got saved—August 20, 1994.

In the days that followed, my brain was filled with many questions. The one question that kept coming up over and over was, "Why?" Why did He spare *me*? I was disrespectful, rebellious, and prideful, to say the least. So now I asked myself, "What now, God?" How was I supposed to act? How am I to change? This was my mindset for the next few months.

What came a few months later brought out my desperate cry even more. On October 29 of that same year, fourteen federal agents armed with guns and bulletproof vests raided our business. It was one of those moments you never forget. You remember every detail of the day—what you were wearing, who you were with, and what you were doing. It was very traumatic for me. Even though the end result was in our favor, it altered my life forever. The event just added to the many wounds deep within me.

In 1994 my brokenness became unbearable. My wounds were eating me alive inside. I became paranoid, frantic, confused, and fearful. I thank the Lord that He found me just in time. God knows our hearts. He knew I had hit rock bottom and was desperately crying out to Him to save me. He came to rescue me and saved me from my brokenness. As I felt His love for me, I wanted more and more of Him.

Why am I telling you all this? Because I want you to know that this experience has caused me to become so desperate for Him that nothing else matters. I wanted to desperately live with Him and not die without Him. Out of this desperation came this insatiable hunger that would never go away.

Hunger Pains

Have you ever woken up in the middle of the night with your stomach rumbling? Your body is telling you that you need food. Your response is to get up out of bed and get something to eat. Ignoring your hunger pains makes it hard to go back to sleep. Then when you get that perfect snack, you are satisfied, and fall asleep easily. Morning comes, and you find that you are hungry again, so you eat breakfast. Our bodies need food or nourishment to survive. If we don't respond to our hunger pains, we will eventually get sick and die.

You can look at this from a spiritual standpoint also. Just like your stomach becomes hungry, your spirit becomes hungry. Your spirit is crying out for food, longing to be fed. Our spirit needs food.

> But He answered and said, "It is written, man shall not live by bread alone, but by every word that proceeds from the mouth of God." (Matthew 4:4)

How do we know our spirit is hungry? When you first meet Jesus, you want to know everything about Him and His kingdom. You start to feel drawn to Him. You want to be with Him and worship Him. You

Chapter 9: The Desperate Cry

feel a tug to open your Bible and begin to talk with Him to cultivate a relationship. This relationship feeds your hunger, the kind of hunger in your spirit that causes you to draw near to Him. It is insatiable. It is like you can't get enough of Him. But you can. When you feed on Him, you will be satisfied. Just like you need food every day for your physical body to stay healthy and nourished, you need spiritual food every day to grow and be strengthened in Him.

> Blessed *are* those who hunger and thirst for righteousness, for they shall be filled. (Matthew 5:6)

Stages of Revelation

My life changed forever that hot August day when I gave my life over to Jesus Christ. I started to see how much He loved me. It wasn't one of those experiences where I had a complete changeover from my old lifestyle; He had to do a work in me. Yes, I had a wake-up call that day, and I became desperate for Him. I became hungry to learn more of Him. I carried my Bible with me wherever I went while I smoked marijuana. God and pot were what I lived for at that time. I preached about Jesus to whoever would listen. Then one day, the Lord revealed Himself to me, and that was the day I quit smoking marijuana. That moment changed my life forever.

As we feed and nourish our relationship with God, it is during these precious moments when He reveals Himself to us. We begin to learn and grow in Him. He teaches and shows us things that will guide us into what He created us for.

> For the word of God *is* living and powerful, and sharper than any two-edged sword, piercing even to the division of soul and spirit, and of joints and marrow, and is a discerner of the thoughts and intents of the heart. (Hebrews 4:12)

He is such an awesome Father. Earthly fathers nourish and guide their children as they are growing. When a baby is born, the father bonds and creates a loving relationship so the child knows they are safe and loved.

A child grows in stages. They learn to crawl before they can walk, they babble before they learn to talk, and they drink milk before they can eat solid foods. Just as a young infant bonds with their parents, we have to learn to bond with our heavenly Father. As this bonding is taking place, we are cultivating a relationship of love and learning to trust in Him. God begins to reveal little tidbits of Himself little by little so we can learn to walk, talk, and eat solid foods as we are growing and maturing in Him.

> **Like a child, we grow in stages. God begins to reveal little tidbits of Himself little by little so we can learn to walk, talk, and eat solid foods as we are growing and maturing in Him.**

That was what He was doing in my life. When I became desperate for Jesus, I wanted to learn more about Him. I was immature and couldn't let the things go that made me feel satisfied in this world. I had to learn how to walk, talk, and eat all over again like a newborn baby.

So why does the Lord give us small snippets of revelation and not everything all at once? First, He knows we wouldn't be able to handle everything He wants to give us, and secondly, He wants us to keep going after Him. He leaves a trail of breadcrumbs for us to follow. Sometimes He will make the breadcrumbs a little bit of a challenge for us to find. And sometimes He wants to play hide and seek with us. He doesn't actually want to hide from us; He wants us to find Him. Finding Him increases our hunger. Remember, this kind of hunger causes Him to give us more revelation of Himself.

CHAPTER 9: THE DESPERATE CRY

When God gives us more revelation, it's because He wants to give us a greater understanding of just how good He really is. God is good! That's a revelation in itself. Truly discovering who God really is has more value than any earthly treasure. The revelation of Jesus Christ is the greatest revelation known to man because it demonstrates the greatest depth of love that God revealed through His Son for us.

> That Christ may dwell in your hearts through faith; that you, being rooted and grounded in love, may be able to comprehend with all the saints what is the width and length and depth and height—to know the love of Christ which passes knowledge; that you may be filled with all the fullness of God. (Ephesians 3:17-19)

In these verses, we can see that God wants us to walk into the fullness that He has for each and every one of us, but it is impossible to walk into that fullness without understanding how much Jesus Christ really loves us. Just catching a glimpse of His great love helps us understand the way we're supposed to love. This type of unconditional love may seem impossible with man, but all things are possible with God. After all, Jesus Christ is the Pattern Son.

The Choice

In God's desire for His children to come to Him, God made sure that He does not force us to love or honor Him. Because He wants us to freely come to Him, He leaves it up to us. He gives us a choice in the matter. Rather than creating robot-like subjects programmed to do things, God built free will into every human being.

> Behold, I stand at the door and knock. If anyone hears My voice and opens the door, I will come in to him and dine with him, and he with Me. (Revelation 3:20)

Many people ask questions like, "Why would God allow bad things to happen to people?" or "Why doesn't God just create people to already do the right thing?" But think about it; if He didn't give us the freedom to choose Him, it wouldn't really be love.

Have you ever been in a relationship where you felt as though the person only acknowledged or loved you when you did what they wanted? It's not a fun time for the person on the serving side of things! In our mixed-up world, sometimes we get thrown into situations where we are forced to be around people who clearly don't want to have anything to do with us—or who we don't want to have anything to do with. Like those strained family reunions with the family member you can't stand, at best, you end up merely tolerating each other for the sake of keeping the peace.

This isn't the kind of relationship God wants with any of His children. He doesn't want us to feel like we are forced to spend time with Him. How would you feel if your loved one expressed that they wanted to be anywhere else but with you and made whatever excuses they could to do literally anything else? It would feel pretty horrible, right?

But that's exactly what some of us do to God. We make excuses for not reading His Word (His Love Letter to us), not going to church, and not praying. Then when we do these things, we keep track of the time, just waiting for the minute when we feel like we've given Him enough time and can move on to the "more important" things in our day. How sad!

Now think of someone who wants to be around you. Maybe they call and text, or just want to spend time with you. It's a good feeling, right? When we fall in love with our spouse, we count the minutes until we get to see them and talk to them again. This is the type of relationship God wants with us, and He gives us the free will to want to build our relationship with Him. It's that free will to accept Jesus that lets us decide how deep we want to go with God.

> O God, You *are* my God; early will I seek You; my soul thirsts for You; my flesh longs for You in a dry and thirsty land where there is no water. So I have looked

CHAPTER 9: THE DESPERATE CRY

for You in the sanctuary, to see Your power and Your glory. (Psalm 63:1-2)

Keeping Passion Alive

Do you remember when you first met your spouse? Remember the burning desire you had for each other? You wanted to spend every waking minute together—you were passionately in love. Sadly, many relationships today lose the spark way too quickly. Careers, hobbies, and self-interests cause many couples to become distant from each other. "The honeymoon period," as we know it, becomes a thing of the past. We live our lives day in, day out just to make it through another day. Sometimes we get so wrapped up in our own lives that we forget we have a "better half."

Any marriage counselor will tell you that it takes work to keep love and passion alive through years and decades of a marriage relationship. To keep love alive, it takes determination, focus, and creativity so boredom doesn't set in.

> **It brings joy to God when we freely choose to do things that help our relationship with Him to grow and thrive.**

When we're around someone for a long time and get comfortable with that person, there's a tendency for us to become bored and complacent. Some people call this the "couch-potato syndrome." It's not wrong to be comfortable around them, but when it starts to affect our relationship, that's when we need to become proactive about pushing aside the laziness that threatens to put a damper on the relationship.

This is another step in our free will; it's our choice to either grow our relationship with God or do things to bring it down—just like in interpersonal relationships. It brings joy to God when we freely choose to do things that help our relationship with Him to grow and thrive.

> Jesus answered and said to him, "If anyone loves Me, he will keep My word; and My Father will love him, and We will come to him and make Our home with him." (John 14:23)

What's amazing about the Lord is that He will continue to pursue us—*even when we push Him away*. No matter what we do in life, even if we sin or turn our back on Him, He will continually cry out for us to come back to Him. His love for us is unconditional, never stopping, never waning. He never gets bored in His love for us!

Yielding to the Cry

Deep down, every human being has a need—a desire—that can only be filled by God. Many people try to fill it with so many other things, but it can only be met by having that thriving relationship with our Creator. And no matter how far or close we are to Him, He continues to cry out for us to draw closer.

Can you hear it? Can you feel it? He yearns and longs for you to be close to Him, just like those who fall in love are consumed by thoughts of their beloved. There is a cry that comes from the Father to you, as well as a cry from your heart reaching out to God.

So why do we sometimes fail to hear the cry? Perhaps our busy lives push Him right out of it. We have so much going on that time with God gets stamped with a low-priority label. It can be easy to do because it's an invisible thing that's easy for some people to fake. We say our relationship with God is great when in reality, everything else in our day takes precedence over it.

It takes a conscious effort to make sure that having time with God becomes the first priority of our day, and not just as an item on a list to be checked off for the day. Personally, I have come to a place in my life

Chapter 9: The Desperate Cry

where I can't imagine starting the day off without sitting in the presence of God for a few hours. It's more than just a habit for me; it's a lifeline!

When we determine to put aside all the distractions, that's when we can best hear God's voice calling out to us. And it's the step of yielding to that cry that's the most important. We stuff down our own desperate cry to the Father by filling our lives with all sorts of things in a vain attempt to fill the void, only to find that He is the only one who could satisfy that deep need.

David wrote about this deep cry:

> As the deer pants for the water brooks, so pants my soul for You, O God. My soul thirsts for God, for the living God. When shall I come and appear before God?....Deep calls unto deep at the noise of Your waterfalls; All Your waves and billows have gone over me. (Psalm 42:1-2,7)

In this passage, David is talking about a passion that has yet to be fulfilled. He came to a place of desperate longing for God's presence. When we come to the place of complete surrender, that's when we truly realize how much we need God as more than just a way out of trouble, but as an intricate part of our daily lives.

The Spirit cries out for you to return to Him. You may not even be far from God, just a bit bored or complacent. He calls out for you to return to Him.

Chapter 10: Finding First Love

Infatuation or True love?

Do you remember the day you said yes to Jesus? The day you gave your life to Him and accepted Him as your personal Lord and Savior? Go back and think about that day for a moment. Remember the emotions? How did you react? What did you feel? For me, I was undone. He accepted me for who I was. I was a broken man with sin, trauma, and pain. I was blown away that He would accept me.

There are many important events that mark the timeline of life. Remember the first time you rode your bike without training wheels? That took courage! Remember your first kiss? A special day to never forget. How about a memorable trip? What about marriage or the birth of a child? And yet, as wonderful as all of these events are, they pale in comparison to that day when Jesus came into our lives. How can that be? Because He becomes our first—our first love, our first everything. He becomes our whole world.

For some of us, we become infatuated with Jesus. It may start out as a strong, passionate feeling for Him and then fades away over time. We may think about Him and continue to carry that love for Him, but the emotions we experienced when we first met Him tend to lessen. We may continue to walk with Him and talk with Him, but it becomes a second thought. What once was a priority now becomes secondary.

The King's Bridal Company

To be in love with Jesus means you are in relationship with Him. Do you remember your first crush or the first time you fell in love with someone? You were probably excited to just look at them. You could stare at them for hours and be so mesmerized by their appearance. That's what it is like when we first fall in love with Jesus. We want to just stare at His face and be mesmerized by His beauty. We could spend hours soaking in His presence because we can't get enough of Him. Jesus is so mesmerized by you and so in love with you. When we worship Him and put Him first, He can't get enough of us.

Growing up in a religious household and attending a religious school was all I ever knew as a child. I memorized repetitious prayers, followed religious traditions, and practiced what I thought were the ways of the Lord. But I had no idea who He really was. I didn't have a clue that He wanted to know me in a personal way. The truth is that He cares about us and wants us to make Him the center of our existence; not so He can rule or govern our lives, but so He can set us free from religion and rules that govern us. Religion can get in the way of us knowing Him the way He wants us to. We need to get to that place where nothing gets in the way.

> **The love you have for your spouse, children, or parents should not be comparable to the love you have for your heavenly Father.**

He is your first love and takes precedence over all other relationships. The love you have for your spouse, children, or parents should not be comparable to the love you have for your heavenly Father. When you said yes to Him, you were putting Him first in your life above everything else. He wants to be number one! Put away the things you worship or adore in this life, things that may become your idol. Our God is a jealous God. He wants you to only worship and adore Him. Put away earthly

Chapter 10: Finding First Love

desires and desire only Him. Our focus should be solely on Jesus, our first true love.

When you do these things and put Jesus first, you'll be amazed at what happens in your life! Try it and see. Wonderful, incredible things will begin to happen. Things that you once thought impossible will now be attainable, all because you decided to put Him first and treasure Him above all else.

> Delight yourself also in the Lord, and He shall give you the desires of your heart. (Psalm 37:4)

The Wooing

Some people say that when they came to know the Lord, they "found Jesus." But it's really the other way around. What's so amazing about our God, our Lover, is that He is the one who finds us first. It's not us finding Him—He finds us!

I had an incredible experience once that showed me just how much Jesus is drawn to us. I was praying in the Spirit and was caught up in a trance, and the Holy Spirit took me into what was a well-known retail store. I was walking around the store when I noticed a man sitting on a bench. There were many people bustling around the store, but nobody noticed the man on the bench. It was like he was invisible to them. But not me. I noticed him right away, and I couldn't stop staring at him. He was smiling at me and began to motion with his finger for me to come closer. I felt so drawn to him because there seemed to be something familiar about him. I couldn't resist moving toward him. As I walked closer, my eyes never left his. As soon as I got up to him, I immediately knew it was the Lord. He was Jesus! I knew it was Him just by His presence, and He was strikingly beautiful! I was so mesmerized by Him. He couldn't stop staring at me. He reached out to hug me, and I fell into his arms, sobbing uncontrollably. Then the encounter was over. I didn't want it to end. What an experience!

The King's Bridal Company

When I reflect on this encounter, I am amazed at how much He loves us. Here I was, rushing around in my life (the store), and He took the time to sit right in front of me (He found me). There were many people in the store, but nobody else noticed Him. They were too busy to stop and look. But He was there all the while and always is. He will keep pursuing us—wooing us to come closer.

No matter what your past looks like, no matter how far away you may feel from God, He will still pursue you. It doesn't matter what you've done; He loves you anyway! And He will pull out all the stops when it comes to reaching out to His children to prove His love. He already did that through the crucifixion.

Sometimes people feel like they have to get their life cleaned up before God will accept them, but this is a religious misconception that has been passed down generation after generation. Even the prodigal son thought his father would never accept him as his own child after the way he had dishonored his wealth and inheritance. When he had spent everything and was completely at the end of the rope, he decided to slink back home, memorizing a speech about how he wasn't worthy to be called a son anymore. But look at the father's response:

> But when he was still a great way off, his father saw him and had compassion, and ran and fell on his neck and kissed him. And the son said to him, "Father, I have sinned against heaven and in your sight, and am no longer worthy to be called your son."
>
> But the father said to his servants, Bring out the best robe and put *it* on him, and put a ring on his hand and sandals on *his* feet. And bring the fatted calf here and kill *it,* and let us eat and be merry; for this my son was dead and is alive again; he was lost and is found." (Luke 15:20-24)

God the Father is just like the father in the parable; He is waiting, longing for you to come back to Him. And nothing you could ever do will change the love He has for you! The father in the story wasn't

Chapter 10: Finding First Love

ignorant; even the older son knew how his brother had been living. I'm sure word had gotten back to the family while he was gone, and people made comments to the father like, "If you only knew what your son was doing," as they shook their heads sadly.

But the father would have none of it; He pushed aside their comments and went back to the window, watching and waiting for his beloved son to return. He knew one day his boy would be back—and there was nothing on earth that would keep him from missing that moment! He waited by the door, watching in the distance, knowing that his beloved son would be back anytime. The verse says that the son was still a long way off, and the father knew that it was him coming home. The son didn't have the clothing that he'd left with—he was dirt poor! How did that dad know it was his boy? Most likely, he had memorized his son's gait, recognizing him by how he walked and his height and hair color. It was him! He rushed out to embrace him, welcoming him home with open arms.

This is how much the Father loves us too. He knows our past trauma and sins; He knows the motives of our heart and how we are not always acting with purity and devotion to Him—and yet He still pursues us.

> # He not only will pursue you, but He will also set things up in your life in a way that will cause you to *want* to seek Him.

It is in this stage—the wooing stage—when we see the heart of the Bridegroom toward His bride—you! He not only will pursue you, but He will also set things up in your life in a way that will cause you to *want* to seek Him. You will begin to feel something drawing you to the presence of the Lord. You may not even be able to explain why or what the motivation is—you just know that you have to be in His presence. It's like what happens when you begin to fall in love with someone. You want to be with them, and you think about them all the time throughout the day.

At the same time that this is happening, don't be surprised if there are many things that try to steal your attention away from the Lord—don't allow it! Guard that time with Him; it is a precious thing that needs to be nurtured and developed, just like any other relationship. He wants you to fall head over heels in love with Him!

Worship

For the believer who is falling in love with Jesus, worship should flow naturally. It's the deep cry of our spirit reaching out to our Maker, surrendering all and showing our devotion.

When we mention worship, many people think about singing songs in church on Sunday. That is part of our corporate worship, lifting Jesus high when we gather with other people. But, believe it or not, most of our worship doesn't even involve singing! It is more about the attitude of our heart tilted heavenward throughout every part of our day rather than just singing songs in a certain location at a specific time.

> **Believe it or not, most of our worship doesn't even involve singing!**

When Jesus was speaking to the woman at the well in John chapter 4, she made reference to a certain place where the people should go to worship. Jesus' response to her was revolutionary—especially for that day and age. He said,

> Woman, believe Me, the hour is coming when you will neither on this mountain, nor in Jerusalem, worship the Father. You worship what you do not know; we know what we worship, for salvation is of the Jews. But the

Chapter 10: Finding First Love

> hour is coming, and now is, when the true worshipers will worship the Father in spirit and truth; for the Father is seeking such to worship Him. (John 4:21-23)

We're supposed to worship Jesus in Spirit and truth. So what does that look like? It's about living our whole lives to please God. It's making decisions that reflect His character and likeness so that everyone around us will want to fall in love with Him too. It's being the husband, father, wife, mother, etc., who points our family to Jesus, making sure that our words and actions help draw them to the Father's love and not make them want to pull away from Him. It's taking notice of the people and situations around us and shining a light in the darkness just by being present. It's being aware of the spiritual needs of people who might be standing right next to us and being willing to come out of our comfort zone to bridge the gap and be Jesus to the world we live in. That's all worship!

Maybe you're saying, "Sal, that sounds impossible! How can I live a life of worship all the time? I'm not Jesus." Sure, we don't always make the right decisions all the time. But it's more about our intentions and motivations—and being willing to admit when we have been wrong and move quickly to ask for forgiveness.

There are times in all of our lives when worship can become a struggle; it happens. When you feel like you're in that place, you need to take inventory of what you are allowing into your thoughts and heart. What have you been watching or listening to? Are there things that eat away at the moments in your day when you are normally worshipping the Lord, but your focus shifted to other things? It's easy to let a rut become a sinkhole if you aren't careful! Sometimes you can let things into your life that can stop up your well of worship without even realizing it. When you notice this, make sure to take quick action to get these things out of your life and restore that flow of worship. Watch and see how purging those things will bring order to your communion with the Lord.

Adoration

When we talk about worship, other words seem to run in tandem with it, such as *adoration*. Worship and adoration appear to go hand in hand, but they are two different things. Webster defines the word *adore* as, "To love in the highest degree,"[5] whereas he said *worship* has more to do with respect and honor.

I see adoration as a more personal form of worship. It's what we do when others are not around. The personal time we spend sitting at Jesus' feet and pouring out our hearts to Him can be considered adoration.

The personal time we spend sitting at Jesus' feet and pouring out our hearts to Him can be considered adoration.

Unfortunately, it seems to be something that many of us neglect to make much time for. But without these precious moments of adoration, we end up running our spiritual lives on empty.

It's been said many times that you can't give out what you don't already possess. And this is certainly true of the presence of God. In order for Christ's life to be mirrored in your own, you have to be filled up with Him. And to be filled with Him, you need to spend time with Him—time in adoration.

What happens when we do this is phenomenal! He takes our dry hearts and begins pouring His water of life into us. In turn, this not only satisfies the longings that we have, making us not want to turn to worldly pleasures anymore, but it ignites a desire for more and more of His presence. We can't get enough! It becomes a continual well, just like Jesus explained to the woman at the well:

---

5. Webster's Collegiate Dictionary, s.v., "adore," (G. & C. Merriam Co., Springfield, MA: 1913).

Chapter 10: Finding First Love

> But those who drink the water I give will never be thirsty again. It becomes a fresh, bubbling spring within them, giving them eternal life. (John 4:14 NLT)

Our worship—our respect and honor—of God will naturally develop into adoration as we continually seek Him. This progression is similar to how people fall in love with each other. First, we see that other person, and an infatuation develops. Then there comes wooing, when one or both people will turn their attention to each other. As this happens, respect and honor are built, leading to adoration and love. Somewhere along the way, that first physical contact happens; the first kiss.

The Kiss

When a baby is born, our first instinct is to grab hold of him or her and give a kiss. There is nothing like kissing a newborn baby. They have that certain "baby" smell they give off, and babies just have a sweet innocence about them. Every mother and father can relate to this. The first time you hold your new son or daughter, you just gaze upon them with such love and adoration. It feels like your heart could burst open.

When we think about a kiss, there are many reasons why we might kiss someone. It might be precious kisses to a newborn baby, a kiss between a man and a woman, a kiss of a mother's love for her child, a kiss to ease someone's hurt or pain, or a kiss to show joy or happiness. In all of these incidences, one thing is in common—love. A kiss is a way to show someone you care about them, that you love them. Kisses can be soothing, nurturing, affectionate, gentle, or passionate. It is a way to show intimacy—that you connect with the person you are kissing, whether it be on the lips, cheek, forehead, or hand. A kiss can be a way to say, "Welcome! You are loved, accepted, and wanted here in this place."

When we meet Jesus for the first time, He reaches out to us and gives us that first kiss. We lean into Him and feel His love for us. It is a kiss of love. He is like a new parent who wraps us up in His arms and gazes upon us. He waits for us to open our eyes. As we start to "see," we look into the eyes of a loving Father. The kiss washes away our tears and sadness. We are washed clean. We become new. This kiss brings joy and happiness. We feel welcomed into His loving arms. As we go through this experience, we want more. We become hungry for Him.

We want to be with Him more and more. His face becomes so beautiful to us, and we want to snuggle in His arms. He becomes a sense of comfort. We want more of His sweet fragrance.

Have you ever had a fragrance that you loved—fresh washed towels or sheets, perfume, or flowers? The smell attracts you. With the attraction comes a calming, relaxing, or soothing feeling. We are attracted to Jesus' fragrance because of what He gives us. He gives us that calming, relaxing, soothing feeling. He gives us peace.

With a kiss comes intimacy. Jesus wants us to have an intimate relationship with Him. He wants us to put Him first. He wants us to worship, adore Him, and glorify His name. Intimacy brings closeness. When you are intimate with someone, it means it is private. God wants us to go to Him in private. In our secret place. He wants us to be laid-down lovers to Him. We don't have to wait for Jesus to kiss us. We can go to Him and kiss Him.

> **With a kiss comes intimacy. Jesus wants us to have an intimate relationship with Him. He wants us to put Him first.**

Let Jesus know that your love for Him is unwavering. Be like that little kid you once were who can't wait for your daddy to come home so you can be with Him. Go to Him. Play with Him. He's waiting for you!

Heaven Kisses Earth

In the physical realm, a kiss is a point of contact that holds great meaning between the two parties involved, whether it is a family

Chapter 10: Finding First Love

relationship or an intimate one. In the same way, there are moments in time when heaven touches earth, and they meet in a type of spiritual "kiss."

One very significant time when this happened was when Jesus died. At that instant, the veil in the temple split in two—from top to bottom. We have all heard this many times, but when you look at what really transpired, it is life-changing!

For those who don't know, the veil in the temple separated the most intimate place where the presence of God dwelled, the holy of holies, from the rest of the temple. The veil (which was actually several inches thick) tore all the way, starting at the top and through to the very bottom, signifying that heaven was coming down to "kiss" earth. The veil was torn from top to bottom—from heaven to earth.

No longer did anyone have to go through rules and rituals and priests to reach God—He is accessible to everyone. On top of that, when the Holy Spirit came, every person can have supernatural experiences and encounters if they know how to reach that "holy place" in God. Sadly, most people don't know how to live in that special place where they can access the supernatural, let alone know how to enter.

On top of forgiveness and His presence and everything that goes with it, there is a whole realm of the supernatural that can be tapped into. It's when you come into this "holy place" in the spirit where the believer can have visionary and supernatural experiences on a regular basis. Unfortunately, a large number of people don't know how to live in the holiest place. In my estimation, ninety-five percent or more of all people never get to that stage.

In later books, I plan to write more about how to get into that holiest place in the spirit realm, but for the sake of this book, I want to encourage you to never stop pressing in and going to deeper places in God. You will never find the end of it. You can go from glory to glory every day.

The King's Bridal Company

Once we have fallen in love with Jesus and we experience that "kiss," a shift happens in our thinking, and this is what I want to talk about in the next chapter.

Chapter 11: Snow White

There's another level in God that we arrive at after we come to Jesus and walk through those first initial stages of falling in love with Him. We don't look at things the way we used to. We see the world around us differently. We look at other people differently—it completely transforms us! Let's walk through the process of how this happens.

Drenched in Love

After salvation, as long as someone continues growing in the things of the Lord, every person will get to a point where maturity happens and the relationship deepens. By this time, we are fully in love with Jesus, and He has totally overwhelmed us with His love—we are soaking wet, fully drenched in the Father's love for us! The Bible has a lot to say about this great, undying love that God has for His bride, His children—you! Here are just a few:

> Understand, therefore, that the Lord your God is indeed God. He is the faithful God who keeps his covenant for a thousand generations and lavishes his unfailing love on those who love him and obey his commands. (Deuteronomy 7:9 NLT)

> For the Lord your God is living among you. He is a mighty savior. He will take delight in you with gladness. With his love, he will calm all your fears. He will rejoice over you with joyful songs. (Zephaniah 3:17 NLT)

> For the mountains may move and the hills disappear, but even then my faithful love for you will remain. My covenant of blessing will never be broken," says the Lord, who has mercy on you. (Isaiah 54:10)

These verses don't even cover everything Jesus said about how He loves us, let alone the fact that Christ died so we can have our sins removed and be in fellowship with God.

When you get hold of that amazing love, it is mind-blowing! I think about all the terrible things I've done, and it makes me wonder How in the world God could even want to be near me, let alone want me as His child or bride.

When we come to know Christ, we don't necessarily know how to love God back. Sure, we know that He loves us, but we may not know exactly how to reciprocate that to Him. There's great value in learning how to cry out to the Lord, "Teach me how to love You!" And as we allow that cry to well up within us, He will be right there to show us the way.

Another thing that happens when we are drenched in God's life-changing love is that we have an increasing desire to constantly remain pure. When the enemy throws temptations our way in every area of life, as he always does, the more we are soaked in the intimate love of God, the less we will have a desire to allow our heart to be led astray by those things and purity will become a higher priority for us.

Power in the Blood

There is a great realization that comes the more we stay in God's love, and that is how powerful the blood of Jesus is! Before coming to this stage, the blood may not have held much significance for us. In

Chapter 11: Snow White

spite of singing songs and hearing sermon after sermon about the blood and its power, until we have learned how much of an impact it can make on every part of our lives to return to the cross continually, it won't mean much.

So just what is it about the blood that we need to learn?

First of all, we come to realize that the blood purifies. It washes our sin away and makes us pure again. All day, every day, we are barraged with things that try to pull our attention away from our Lord. We are tempted to do and think things we shouldn't—and sometimes we won't always be strong enough to resist. How wonderful that the blood of Jesus is there to wash over us and make us clean again.

> But if we walk in the light as He is in the light, we have fellowship with one another, and the blood of Jesus Christ His Son cleanses us from all sin. (1 John 1:7)

The next thing the blood does is to protect. After we are cleansed from sin, we need to remain under the fountain of the blood of Jesus, allowing it to constantly keep our mind pure—taking every thought captive—and it will help protect us from future attacks on our hearts and minds.

> **After we are cleansed from sin, we need to remain under the fountain of the blood of Jesus, allowing it to constantly keep our mind pure.**

Next we find that the blood saves us. It saves us from ourselves and from the world. It saves us from sickness and pain because there is healing that comes through the blood of Jesus. First Peter 2:24 says that we are healed by His stripes that He bore on the cross.

Another thing the blood does is it justifies. It not only cleanses us from sin, but when God looks at us, He sees the blood of Jesus and it's just as though we had never even sinned! What an amazing gift! Romans 3:24-25 says,

> All are justified freely by his grace through the redemption that came by Christ Jesus. God presented Christ as a sacrifice of atonement, through the shedding of his blood—to be received by faith. He did this to demonstrate his righteousness, because in his forbearance he had left the sins committed beforehand unpunished

What's even more wonderful is that the blood of Jesus can actually draw us closer to the Lord. Ephesians 2:13 says, "But now in Christ Jesus you who once were far off have been brought near by the blood of Christ." What a picture of a cleansing cycle. We see the blood and are drawn to it; which in turn purifies, protects, saves, and justifies us. The more we dwell in that place, the less we will want to leave.

The blood brings a total mind transformation. As we realize its significance and the ultimate sacrifice that Jesus made so that we can have access to the power in His blood, something happens. An identity shift begins to happen as we see who we really are in Christ—we are a son or daughter of the King. Then we come to another level in our love and commitment to our Lord—one of no compromise.

No Compromise

As we grow in our relationship with Jesus, there comes a time when, as the bride of Christ, we get to a place where we will not compromise. And this doesn't just apply to sinful worldly desires; it encompasses many things.

As we walk through the growing levels of our relationship with God, don't be surprised if there are offers for better positions, more money, more material possessions, and things like that. The enemy likes to take things that dazzle us in the world and dangle it in front of us to try and

Chapter 11: Snow White

draw us away from God. This is what He did to Jesus when he was tempting Him. The enemy even offered to give Jesus all the kingdoms of the world and their splendor. But Jesus saw through his deceit and countered back with the Word of God.

You might get something promised to you on a silver platter; it might even be something you thought that you needed or have wanted for a long time, but in order to have those things, you will end up compromising your time and relationship with the Lord. Don't do it! God is looking for those who will be completely devoted to Him, and He wants to be in the center of everything we do—and it's for our benefit when we live this way! God has good plans for us.

Make a determination now that no matter how big your platform gets, no matter how well-known or wealthy you become, that you find your identity in Christ—not in all those things that people in the world would say are important and defining. Make the decision ahead of time that you will not compromise your faith for the sake of anything else. And when your identity is wrapped up in the fact that you are a lover of God, it makes it that much easier not to compromise your faith when the enemy dangles that "carrot" in front of your face.

> **Make the decision ahead of time that you will not compromise your faith for the sake of anything else.**

Walking Out the Beatitudes

We talked earlier in-depth about the Beatitudes, but we see it here again. Through this process, those in the Bridal Company will also learn how to walk in the Beatitudes. In doing this, they learn that they are just and righteous. They become determined not to compromise or "sell out." Just look at the rewards that are given for hungering after God, staying pure, and keeping peace, among everything else!

The King's Bridal Company

> Blessed are the poor in spirit, for theirs is the kingdom of heaven. Blessed are those who mourn, for they will be comforted. Blessed are the meek, for they will inherit the earth. Blessed are those who hunger and thirst for righteousness, for they will be filled. Blessed are the merciful, for they will be shown mercy. Blessed are the pure in heart, for they will see God. Blessed are the peacemakers, for they will be called children of God. Blessed are those who are persecuted because of righteousness, for theirs is the kingdom of heaven. (Matthew 5:3-10 NIV)

As a child of God, there will be many opportunities on a daily basis to walk out the Beatitudes. Just think back over the last week, and notice the decisions you had that line up with the verses above. Were there times when you needed to keep the peace in a situation, maybe holding your own tongue to keep peace when you wanted to rip into someone? What about a chance to show someone mercy when they didn't deserve it? How about times when you could push aside social media and television in order to spend time hungering and thirsting for more of the Lord? What about purity of heart? The list goes on and on.

Those who long to be snow-white in the Lord will want to be conformed to the life of walking out the Beatitudes. They will realize that they really are poor in spirit—so destitute without the presence of God living and breathing and moving through them—that they will walk into the kingdom of God without restraint.

And yet, twenty chapters later, Jesus comes along and gives us a parable that, at first glance, doesn't seem to have much of a connection with the Beatitudes, but it really does. Let me explain.

The Ten Virgins

We've all heard the parable of the ten virgins so many times that we could probably recite it from memory. There are five wise virgins who are prepared with oil for their lamps and five foolish ones who didn't

Chapter 11: Snow White

bring enough oil and miss out on the coming of the bridegroom when they have to leave to get their refills.

I have mostly heard this parable interpreted as the five foolish virgins being compared to people who miss out on Jesus' return and don't make it into heaven. This is the way many people see this parable, and that is how I used to see it as well.

The awesome thing about having a close, intimate relationship with Father God is that He can at any time change your perspective on how you see things. If you seek Him on things you would like to have more knowledge of, He will give you a deeper understanding along with wisdom and revelation so you can see things in a different light. Scripture can have different levels of meaning, depending on how you look at it. I believe that God has given me further insight on my understanding of this particular scripture of the ten virgins.

Let's take a deeper look.

> Then the kingdom of heaven shall be likened to ten virgins who took their lamps and went out to meet the bridegroom. Now five of them were wise, and five *were* foolish. Those who *were* foolish took their lamps and took no oil with them, but the wise took oil in their vessels with their lamps. But while the bridegroom was delayed, they all slumbered and slept. (Matthew 25:1-5)

Notice that right from the start, ALL of them are virgins. They are all described as being pure. The parable doesn't say that there were five virgins, and then a different term is used to describe the other five. I believe that all ten of these virgins represent people who are saved.

Let's take a look at the rest of the parable:

> And at midnight a cry was *heard:* "Behold, the bridegroom is coming; go out to meet him!" Then all those virgins arose and trimmed their lamps. And the foolish said to the wise, "Give us *some* of your oil, for

our lamps are going out." But the wise answered, saying, "*No*, lest there should not be enough for us and you; but go rather to those who sell, and buy for yourselves." And while they went to buy, the bridegroom came, and those who were ready went in with him to the wedding; and the door was shut.

Afterward the other virgins came also, saying, "Lord, Lord, open to us!" But he answered and said, "Assuredly, I say to you, I do not know you." (Matthew 25:6-12)

It is my opinion that the oil represents the Holy Spirit. I also believe that it represents intimacy. Without a deep relationship with the Spirit of the Lord, there would be no intimacy. It is the Holy Spirit that draws us to our lover. Five of the virgins were in an intense love affair with God. Their lamps were full, which again tells me that they were so full of the Spirit that they were overflowing. The scripture tells us that all the virgins trimmed their lamps and that the foolish virgins' lamps were going out—their fire was going out. Because they didn't cultivate an intimate relationship with the Lord through the Holy Spirit, their flame, or their desire for Him, was waning. We can be saved like the foolish virgins and have a knowledge of God, but it takes a deep, intimate love affair to truly know who our lover really is. The wise virgins were the ones who were so in love with Him, that they were ready and waiting for their bridegroom to come.

Notice that there is a hunger in the five foolish virgins who didn't bring the oil. They saw from the five wise that their lamps were overflowing with the Spirit of God and they wanted it! They desired something that one could only have by paying a steep price. You have to give up things in order to cultivate that vibrant, thriving love affair with Him.

So if they really wanted a relationship with God like that, what was stopping them? There are distractions in life that cause us to waste precious time. We waste so much time going around the

Chapter 11: Snow White

mountain when our lover is right in front of us. Time is of the essence! *Time*.

We waste so much time going around the mountain when our lover is right in front of us. Time is of the essence!

To have a deep relationship with someone, you have to spend significant *time* with them. Those five foolish virgins got the wake-up call of their lifetime! They actually thought they had all the time in the world and instead, got caught up in worldly distractions. The foolish missed it big time! The wise had put the time and effort into spending every possible waking moment with their lover and didn't want to share any of it with them. It is a precious, personal thing that, when you have experienced it, you don't want to give it up for anything!

It is my opinion that in the ages to come there will be a distinction between the Bridal Company and the rest of the church. It is up to you how you will keep your candle burning while you wait for the bridegroom to come. Will you be wise or will you be foolish?

Part 5: Destiny Mirrors

Life is all about preparation. Preparation is a big part of our everyday lives. We prepare for the day by getting showered and dressed. We prepare for the night by making sure the house is secure. We prepare for our studies or our jobs. We prepare for life events like weddings, births, birthdays, graduations, and funerals. We don't realize how much of our lives are filled with preparation. It is a good thing to be prepared because if we aren't, we could get caught off guard and not be ready. Let's all face it. We've all been there a time or two in our lives when we got caught not prepared. Does it bring back memories from your school days when you weren't prepared for that "pop" quiz? One thing is without a doubt in my life—I don't want to be caught off guard when my King Jesus returns. I want to make sure that I'm prepared for His return; I want to be ready. He's coming back for that spotless bride....are you prepared for the King's return?

Yours Forever

The day had finally come. Everything had to be absolutely perfect on their wedding day.

The King's Bridal Company

The king stood at the top of the hill, overlooking what he was about to give to his beautiful bride. He had been preparing for her arrival for quite some time. The waiting seemed like forever, but it was well worth it. The glorious kingdom he created was for such a time as this. She had no idea what lay in store for her.

The king began to daydream about the bride that would soon be his. It wasn't easy to choose her because he knew what she would be acquiring. She had to be a very special bride. Her position meant that she would be elevated in the kingdom. He wanted to choose someone who would love him for who he was, not just for all the riches and status of being married to a king.

He thought about her qualities that drew him to her. She was very rare indeed. She was so full of love for others and always the first one there when someone was in need. His bride-to-be was humble, righteous, and full of wisdom. When something went wrong, she wanted to make it right. In everything she touched, said, or did, good came out. A smile touched his lips just thinking about her. He had chosen well.

The king headed down the hill so he could get ready for his marriage to his long-awaited bride. He couldn't contain his excitement and started to run as if to make the time go faster when he would finally make her his.

The princess bride listened intently as her bridegroom king pledged his love for her. She accepted and pledged her love for him and only him, forever and ever.

"You may kiss your bride," she heard and leaned in with a kiss that would seal their love forever. The wedding between the king and his bride was beyond anything anyone could have imagined.

PART 5: DESTINY MIRRORS

She was the most stunning bride, and all those who laid eyes on her were mesmerized. She was adorned in the most beautiful gown seemingly fit for a king's bride. The gown was made of the purest white silk that shimmered in the sunlight. She was a gorgeous, spotless bride. Yes, she was a beauty on the outside, but something from within her glowed around and through her. Everyone was very happy with their new queen.

The time had arrived for the bridegroom king to give his new bride his marriage gift. He wanted it to be a surprise, so he blindfolded her and whisked her away in their royal carriage.

As they pulled up to the top of the hill, the king asked the driver to stop. He helped his new bride descend from the carriage. Before he took off the blindfold, he stood behind her, held her in his arms, and said, "This gift I give to you from my heart to yours. I have prepared this glorious place for you. My heart has been longing for you to come home to be with your first love and remain with me forever through all eternity." With that, he took the blindfold off.

His new bride gasped at the glory all around her. Tears welled up in her eyes as she began to see what lay ahead of her. The king took her hand, and they walked toward the palace gates. As they approached, she could hear trumpets sounding and voices singing praises to their new king and his bride. She was awestruck. She couldn't believe all this was for her! The palace had walls that were so high they looked like they almost touched the sky. They were made of gold and shone brightly.

As they came upon the palace, she could see that each layer of the foundation was made of precious stones. She suddenly laughed as she noticed that the road heading to the palace was also made of pure gold. As they walked along, she saw a river in the distance that looked like clear crystal. On each side of the river were trees heavy laden with luscious fruit hanging from their branches.

The bridegroom king and his new bride entered the palace, and the new bride was swept away by her bridegroom to their secret place behind closed doors.

As the blissful day ends, she's happy that it's finally just the two of them. The two have now become one in body, soul, and spirit. Never in her wildest dreams could she have ever imagined a gift so rare and beautiful. She was undone. At that moment, the king knew his bride was finally home.

Chapter 12: Waves of Glory

A Day at the Beach

Remember those days as a young child when your mom would yell, "Get your bathing suit on; we are going to the beach!" Ah, beach days! I still reminisce about my time at the ocean as a kid. We packed the car with beach chairs, towels, coolers, and of course, we can't forget the beach toys! I feel the excitement now, thinking about the car ride heading to the beach—window down, the wind blowing in my hair, my shovel in my hand, and a big smile on my face. We pull in, and I can't contain myself as I start running toward the sand. I hear my mom's voice yell, "Sal! Get back here! You need sunblock before you go anywhere, young man!" I chuckle just thinking about it. Of course, I have to reluctantly stop, turn around and head back to my mom to be slathered with lotion.

When I get the go-ahead from mom, I'm off again. My toes hit the sand, and I am one happy kid. I look around to find the perfect spot to build my sandcastle. Not too far, yet not too close to the water. I don't want to be so far that it takes too many trips back and forth from the water to fill my castle moat. I don't want to be too close and take the chance of my castle being trampled on, or, worse yet, the waves crashing in and destroying my castle. I can picture my castle in my head. There are towers, tunnels, windows, and a moat. Those were the days!

As I build my castle with the hot sun shining down on me, I would eventually get very hot and tired. That's when it was time to get in the water to cool off. I set my sand toys down and head to the water. No testing the water for me. Running into the water, I dive in and crash headfirst into the waves, getting immediate relief from my hot, sweaty body. The cool water refreshed and renewed me.

The waves were the best! I loved windy days at the beach because then that meant the waves would be huge. Sometimes the waves would be so big that I could hear my mom yelling at me to be careful. Yes, as a little kid, fear would grip me as I watched a big wave heading toward me. I would wait in anticipation for it to come crashing over me. My toes dug deep into the sand as I watched the wave coming my way. As it hits me, I am knocked down by its powerful force. I get up and can't wait to do it again!

Have you ever been to the beach and pondered how small we really are in this vast world? I have stood on many beaches in my lifetime, and I never get past the feeling of awe as I look out over the never-ending water. Planet earth is mostly covered by oceans. There is so much yet to be discovered in the oceans that we cannot even imagine! Going to the ocean was one of my favorite things to do as a kid and still is today. Now that I am older, it's different. Oh, don't get me wrong—I still love crashing into the waves and letting the powerful force of the waves overtake me.

When I am at the beach, I can see God's glory all around me. It's so beautiful. And that's just what we can see around us. It blows my mind to imagine what is beneath all the water: the plant life, the coral, the fish. I went snorkeling once in Honduras, and the beauty I saw all around me was indescribable—things that didn't seem of this world, the colors, the textures, the life living deep within the ocean. When I go to the beach, I can only think about how God is so good and about the creation He designed for us. So incredibly amazing!

How Deep Will You Go?

> Deep calls unto deep at the noise of Your waterfalls; All Your waves and billows have gone over me. (Psalm 42:7)

Chapter 12: Waves of Glory

As a kid, my mom would freak out if I went out too far in the water, especially when it went over my head. I could never understand it because I love the feeling of swimming out in the deep end. That feeling of not being able to touch the bottom. The freedom to swing and kick your legs freely with no restrictions. Plus, it showed that I wasn't a "baby" anymore, and I could swim in water that was over my head. I was one of the "big kids" now. Yup, that was me. The best part was the feeling of the unknown. It brought a little fear and a bit of excitement, not knowing what was out there or what might come and nibble on my toes. Everyone at one point in their lives experiences going in the "deep end." It may not pertain to an ocean experience, but we all go deep into the unknown at some point. We step out over our heads and wonder what's going to happen next.

That is a feeling we can experience in our walk with Jesus. Many of us have said, "Lord, I may have gotten myself in too deep. What do I do now?" When things get too deep in our lives, we should seek Him. When we are in His presence and flooded with His Spirit, we don't feel overwhelmed, and fear leaves us. The deeper you go, the deeper He takes you in. Going deep can also mean wanting so much of His love that you just want to be in over your head in love with Him. Either way, going into the unknown with Jesus is an experience that will never leave you.

> **When we are in His presence and flooded with His Spirit, we don't feel overwhelmed, and fear leaves us.**

After we take that initial step of accepting Jesus, many of us don't know there's so much more. This includes many leaders who graduated from amazing seminaries and some of the most brilliant theologians on the planet. I'm not knocking anyone, but it's a plain and simple fact. Knowing Him can be separated into knowing Him personally or knowing him intimately. What's the difference, you ask? Well, let's take a look at relationships.

Remember when you started dating? How about getting into a relationship and then finding out that you really don't have anything in common, so you decide to be friends. Or the one you thought might be "the one," but there was something missing. You were yearning for something deeper. And then you meet "the one," and there's no question about it. You know the moment when you fell in love. There was a longing you couldn't explain. There was a sparkle that caught your eye. And then the magic that made everything perfect. It's that moment when the bridegroom meets the bride.

The relationship with Jesus is no different. There are those who know Him because He enlightens us to His existence and they feel content knowing they're saved and still have their life as they want to live it. Then there are those who want a little more, so they begin a relationship with Him but are content to not go deeper. The sense of the unknown is what scares them. And then there are the ones who want Him and only Him. They don't care about anything else but Him. These are the people who function in business or ministry and have learned to live because of His will for their lives. They put Jesus first and foremost above all other things. They are not afraid of the unknown and are willing to go as deep as He will take them. They hunger for the fullness of what He has for them, and it makes them cry out for more and more of Him. It's this cry that moves the magic within Him. It's the cry that brings His gaze upon you and the sparkle in His eye for you. The Bridegroom has found His bride.

This is where the church begins to transform into the bride of Christ, the spotless sold-out-for no-one-else gazing bride who wants nothing more than just Him. I truly believe that thoughts like this move His heart—thoughts of us wanting to just catch a glimpse of Him.

Close your eyes for a moment. Come still before the Lord and ask Him to take all your thoughts captive—every thought you have of your family, your job, your chore list, any distraction that will keep you from seeing His face. Now ask Him to come and flood your mind. Let Him

CHAPTER 12: WAVES OF GLORY

come and flood your mind with His beauty. His incredible joy. Feel His gaze upon you and His love for you. Let His wonderful words wash over your entire being and infuse your spirit. I can only imagine what He is saying about you. He is such an amazing Father who sees us through the eyes of love. Let the peace of His being seep through you and release your worries and burdens to Him.

When I do this, I have a picture in my mind of the greatness of who He is in this universe and all the dimensions within Him that He is still cheering us on as we walk out our journey in life. He is the Conductor in the Great Cloud of Witnesses that are constantly watching us and rooting for us to walk into the fullness that can only be found in Him.

Okay, you can open your eyes again. Wasn't that incredible? We should always want to learn the deeper ways of practicing His presence. There's no such thing as an end to the depth of God. Each experience we have with Him takes us deeper as long as we continue to hunger and want more of Him. It's like that day at the beach, looking out over the water that never seems to end. His desire for us to be with Him is never-ending. There is no depth, height, width, or length within God that can ever be reached. His love for us is beyond measure!

> Oh, the depth of the riches both of the wisdom and knowledge of God! How unsearchable *are* His judgments and His ways past finding out! (Romans 11:33)

The Lord is never ending. He is the everlasting to everlasting. He is the Alpha and the Omega.

Splashed in the Spirit

One morning years ago, I was practicing His presence while I was in contemplative prayer. While praying in the Spirit, I was caught up by the Spirit of God. What an amazing experience I had! From a distance, I saw a beautiful body of water. I wanted to go closer to the water, so the Holy Spirit brought me closer. I then saw elaborate, beautiful yachts a distance out from the shoreline. As I got closer to the shoreline, I started seeing waves. There they were—big, beautiful waves. I hovered over the waves, and they were magnificent! As I approached the beach, a massive wave came and splashed me. I was caught up in the Spirit, and I actually felt the splash and power of the wave! I know you are wondering if I was actually wet when I came back from my wild joy ride with the wonderful Holy Spirit, but no, I wasn't. The cool thing was that while I was in the Spirit, I felt like I was drenched when the wave splashed over me. I asked the Lord, "What was that? It was incredible!" His response was that He would begin splashing me with waves of glory. That was an experience I will never forget!

These waves of glory will not be taught or felt in a religious atmosphere; they only come from being drenched in His presence and spending hours captivated by His awe of us; by intentionally seeking His face and wanting more and more of just Him.

> *When You said,* "Seek My face," My heart said to You, "Your face, Lord, I will seek." (Psalm 27:8)

Wanting just Him is the key to opening the door to a realm full of splendor and power. Nothing more. Nothing less. He is the all in all, everything that we need—just Him. Just like an ocean wave can sometimes catch you off guard, so can being captivated by the thought of just Him.

Wanting just Him is the key to opening the door to a realm full of splendor and power. Nothing more. Nothing less.

Let's look at something. When we talk about water in the prophetic, we can often relate that to washing and cleansing. Prophetically speaking, water can represent the Word. Water washes away debris and makes things clean. We can use the Word to wash, cleanse, and teach

Chapter 12: Waves of Glory

us. The Word of God can become such a big part of your life that it consumes you sometimes. It washes over you and cleanses your entire being—your spirit, soul, and body.

What I mean by "consuming you" is allowing it to penetrate the innermost parts of who you are. The Word of God starts to come alive within you, and it's no longer something educational or boring. You begin to see how useful and powerful the Word of God becomes in your everyday life.

> For the word of God *is* living and powerful, and sharper than any two-edged sword, piercing even to the division of soul and spirit, and of joints and marrow, and is a discerner of the thoughts and intents of the heart. (Hebrews 4:12)

In Ephesians, there is an amazing passage about wives and husbands that I will dive deeper into in the next chapter, but Ephesians 5:26 talks about the church being sanctified and cleansed by the washing of the water by the Word.

Now imagine yourself getting so drenched and filled up by the Word of God that it causes a stirring inside of you. This stirring causes you to want to seek His face and want nothing else. And because of our hunger for Him, it causes the Holy Spirit to stir up a wave that we just get so drenched in His glory. It is in His glory where we find the significance and importance of who He is. He is amazing and all powerful. He is the All in All. There are so many names to describe how awesome He really is!

The Power of the Wave

Let's get back to the beach. When I was a kid, getting splashed by a wave was so much fun! But there were times when I wasn't expecting the wave to hit, catching me off guard because my attention was elsewhere. Those were the most thrilling waves to me. You're not expecting it, and then wham! It hits you like a ton of bricks. When caught off guard, the power of the wave can literally knock you off your feet! When we're in the Word, we can expect to see waves coming toward us, but sometimes we are caught by surprise by how powerful the Word of God can be. We become so engulfed in the Word and in Him that waves of glory just smash into us unexpectedly. I love those moments of being swept off my feet by Him.

Not all waves are the same. They come in all shapes and sizes, which will have an effect on how powerful they hit you. Wind and energy cause waves to form. The size and power of the wave are dependent upon these factors—the more powerful the wind, the more powerful the wave. We can say the same thing about the waves that crash over us when we get into the Word of God. These waves of glory will affect everyone differently. Depending on your walk with God, where you are called to go, and the willingness of how deep you go can make a big difference in the size and power of the wave. Waves of glory are not just for fun. We know how powerful they can be—so powerful that they are splashed on us to transform us into the image of Jesus Christ.

> Beloved, now we are children of God; and it has not yet been revealed what we shall be, but we know that when He is revealed, we shall be like Him, for we shall see Him as He is. And everyone who has this hope in Him purifies himself, just as He is pure. (1 John 3:2-3)

Whether it's a tiny or monstrous wave, everything the Lord sends us is used to conform us into His image. Everything is always about the king, King Jesus.

Riding the Glory

We've experienced getting splashed by the waves, and now it's time to get a little riskier. We get to a point in our lives where we are not content with just swimming and getting splashed by waves. In the distance, we see those monstrous glory waves, and we long to get on one of those waves and take it for a ride. At least that was me.

CHAPTER 12: WAVES OF GLORY

Many years ago, I was so excited to try surfing that I paid a guy to teach me how to surf. He probably thought I would lose patience easily, and then he could move onto his next customer. First of all, you have to wait for just the right wave, which takes time and energy. Learning how to get up on the board is another story. That was difficult. I think the guy was shocked when I actually got up on the board three different times and rode one wave about thirty or forty feet. I was so bummed when he said he had to go. I was just learning how to catch the right wave and having the time of my life!

Now that you understand about taking a risk in the natural and moving from getting splashed by a wave to riding a wave, let's move to what it is like riding a wave of glory in the spirit realm. As we move into our wild ride with waves of glory, there are some things that must take place to sustain and keep us on the wave.

First of all, there are different sizes of waves, so we need to know our limitations. The waves in Australia and Hawaii are different than the waves in Florida. I know every surfer's dream is to hit those big waves, but anything risky can be dangerous. The same goes with the Lord. How many ministries operate in the gifts but don't have the substance to be able to ride the big wave? They can't sustain the ride because their identity is based on performance, and the character and nature of Jesus had never been worked into their lives. How about a prophetic minister who receives revelation and only tries to interpret everything for everyone else, not thinking that the revelation or warning was for himself and not the body?

Here's a rule of thumb I like to follow when it comes to prophesy. First, I always look internally at myself before taking anything I received prophetically to a person or corporately. We must learn that as the Lord moves *through* us, it's also to do a work *in* us. A wave of glory is like a double-edged sword. It is used both inwardly and outwardly. Not only is God dealing with us inwardly, but how we operate outwardly as well.

> He had in His right hand seven stars, out of His mouth went a sharp two-edged sword, and His countenance *was* like the sun shining in its strength. (Revelation 1:16)

As we prepare for riding the wave, we have to learn that the Lord wants us to look inwardly first and foremost. Again, everything that the Lord uses is intended to conform us to the character and nature of Jesus.

It takes strength and stamina to be able to sustain a wave. We need to develop our muscles and be in good shape in order to be on top of that wave. It takes some spiritual muscles and stamina to move with the glory of the wave. Some exercises to build our spiritual strength and stamina include developing a deeper, intimate prayer life, singing in the Spirit, practicing His presence, reading the Word, and soaking in Him through worship. Some others include relationship with fellow believers, spirit-filled books, or classes to nurture our spirit life. There are so many ways to develop your muscles, but whatever you decide, you must be intentional about it. Being intentional brings discipline into our lives. Just like any other strength training, if you stop, you lose shape and get flabby. We lose interest, and before long, we're weak and tired, and things become difficult to do and overcome. It will be very hard to get on and sustain the wave if you don't train your muscles and learn to be consistent.

> Brethren, I do not count myself to have apprehended; but one thing *I do,* forgetting those things which are behind and reaching forward to those things which are ahead, I press toward the goal for the prize of the upward call of God in Christ Jesus. (Philippians 3:13-14)

You must make intimacy with the Father a lifestyle. This is a must. Jesus said He never did anything He didn't see His Father doing. He also said He didn't seek after His own will but the will of the Father. How could He have known what His Father's will was if He wasn't intimate with Him? Intimacy with the Father is the most rewarding treasure we can ever find.

Chapter 12: Waves of Glory

Okay, now that you've built up the strength to climb up on the board, you need balance. Balance takes not only strength but also willpower to stay on the board as long as you can. Balance is the ability to control your strength and endurance. Do you lead a balanced life? Believe it or not, Father God is looking at your life. Is all your strength and endurance focused on your ministry? Where does your family fit in? Are you so worried about the next vison, trance, or dream that you lose focus on the purpose God called you to be? I know I did for a time. It can be so easy to get caught up in the next best thing. We need to be consistent and keep our focus aligned with King Jesus. Give the Lord permission to search your heart. Ask Him where the areas are in your life that you need to give and take to create balance.

> O Lord, You have searched me and known *me*. You know my sitting down and my rising up; You understand my thought afar off. You comprehend my path and my lying down, And are acquainted with all my ways. (Psalm 139:1-3)

The Lord wants you to put Him first above all things and bring a healthy balance to your life. He wants to help you bring that balance. Take a second and look at your life. Do you put Jesus first? Do you spend quality time with your family? What about your ministry or your job?

There was a time in my life when I was so focused on other things that I lost valuable time with my wife and kids. I don't take things for granted anymore. God has shown me the value in my family. The simplest things like helping my wife around the house can bring a sense of balance. It makes me happy knowing that I please my wife. It helps bring balance into her life as well. Ask God to allow Him to show you the things you need to work on. You will feel much better if you follow His direction or will, and not your own.

The greatest balance comes from the Word of God. Without the Word, you have nothing to stand on. Not spending time in the Word means you won't be riding a wave of glory. The Word is your lifeline and is what keeps you sustained on the board. The scriptures will keep your head above water when you are drowning! Immerse yourself in the Word, and you will be amazed at how quickly you learn to climb on the board and balance.

Now you're up and surfing! Congratulations! It takes great strength, skill, and endurance to stay up and ride the wave. We talked about staying in balance, but what about staying in tune? The biggest key is to stay in tune. If we think about a tune in a musical sense, when something goes out of tune, the musical piece becomes a disaster. Staying in tune means to bring into harmony. To stay on the board and ride the wave, we have to align ourselves with the work of the Father in us. We have to stay in harmony with Him. What does that mean? In order to be in tune with Father God, we must let go of our control. We must give ourselves over completely to Him and allow Him to work in us and through us. Your own control without the Father will bring you down. Wanting to abide in Him will help you with your tuning.

> By this we know that we abide in Him, and He in us, because He has given us of His Spirit. (John 4:13)

It's important to know what the Spirit of God is doing and what He is saying. In order to ride a glory wave, you need to let Him take you wherever He wants. He is the wind that causes a stirring in us. He is the energy that powers the wave. He is the awe in the wave that wants to take you for the biggest ride of your life. Whenever you give everything over to Him, you will be on the ride of your life. I've experienced the most incredible waves that the Holy Spirit has taken me on. He has that for you too. Be in expectation to receive the most glorious, exhilarating experience! Always remember that He is with you always, and He is in control!

The Lull

At the beach, I stood and watched as the surfer in the distant ocean was knocked off his board by a giant wave. After a few moments, his head popped up, and he was okay. He climbed back on his board to

Chapter 12: Waves of Glory

search the water for another wave. Paddling back out, he sat on the board and waited.

There's a time period in between waves—a lull. Most people have a hard time with waiting. If you are prophetic, then you probably have struggled with patience at one time or another. I can recall many times when I wanted everything to happen right away. But the Lord knows what's best for us, and He knows the perfect time for our breakthrough. It's in the downtime when the most efficient work can be done.

Imagine we go paddling in the water back to our spot and wait for the next big wave. Picture that wave heading right for us. Now think of that wave as a revelation that comes from the Father and carries glory. Most people who get a revelation receive it and use it externally. They usually don't ever use it internally, so they're never changed from glory to glory. In the lull of the wave, we need to occupy our space until the next wave comes rolling in. The Lord said in Luke 19 that we need to occupy until His return.

> **People want to be able to carry the glory, but we need to allow the Lord to do a work in us during our glorious encounters so we can be sustained to go from glory to glory.**

This waiting in between waves has to be active. Many people get caught up in waiting passively, meaning that they aren't doing anything during their waiting period. They sit and wait for the next wave and then the next without contemplating the last wave. What if the next wave coming upon them can cause a shift within themselves? The Lord is always working on both sides of the fence. As I said before, revelation isn't given just to receive and then turn and give it to others. How you steward the waves of glory you receive depends on the size and depth of the next wave.

The King's Bridal Company

We go from glory to glory. If we can't handle the lull between the waves, then how can we get on the next glory wave? People want to be able to carry the glory, but we need to allow the Lord to do a work in us during our glorious encounters so we can be sustained to go from glory to glory.

As you move on to the next chapter, pretend you are looking into the water. Behold, you may just see a glorious reflection!

> But we all, with unveiled face, beholding as in a mirror the glory of the Lord, are being transformed into the same image from glory to glory, just as by the Spirit of the Lord. (2 Corinthians 3:18)

Chapter 13: Glorious Reflections

We've all hit that crossroad some time or another in our lives where we have to stop and think about where we've been and where we are headed. This experience is different for all of us. For some, life just doesn't stop. It's go, go, go until eventually they crash and burn or simply get lost and forget their purpose. Others go through life slow and steady, cautious at every intersection, making sure they're headed in the right direction. However you look at it, everyone has to come face-to-face with their past at some point. We reflect on things we have gone through—our ups and downs, or the good, bad, and the ugly. We think about what we could have done differently or times that were glorious when we did everything right. One thing is for certain—we will always have a past no matter what we try to do to get rid of it.

What matters is that as long as you are still living and breathing, you still have time to walk into your destiny. But in order to do that, you have to reflect on your life. Many of your reflections might be ones when you didn't act in your best interest or with the greatest attitude. These are the memories you want to forget. Think back on your most embarrassing moment. Remember how you felt? You probably thought to yourself, *I will never do that again!* Or how about a time when you acted out of anger and later regretted it. It's these defining moments that can bring radical change and transformation to a course correction on your path to destiny.

Pondering Thoughts

As we begin to walk in our destiny, there is now another determining moment we need to give full attention to. This moment in time comes when we begin to go deeper and deeper in our search for our lover. We begin to analyze our life as a new creation. We start to ponder and reminisce about our time spent on this earth after we began our walk with God. We look back at where we've been, and forward to where we're going. We know change needs to happen, but where or how?

Reflection brings revelation

Self-reflection is a choice, and it takes discipline. What do I mean by that? For starters, we should be reflecting daily. Most of us already do this when we have our intimate time with the Lord. We thank Him for the good and repent for our mistakes. In these quiet moments with the Father, He speaks to us as our loving Papa. He loves it when we open up our hearts to Him. We can reveal our deepest secrets, and He's there to share them with us. He is there in our sorrows and our joy. We can surrender everything to Him and know that it is taken care of. We can trust in His goodness over our lives and know that it's done and victory is ours.

Not everyone has an easy time facing their past. Some people have a difficult time facing mistakes they've made, or they are so wounded by their past that they block it out completely. I know people who have shoveled so much dirt over their past that it has become deeply buried,—never to be seen again. Out of sight, out of mind. We all know what happens to wounds that don't get taken care of properly. They fester, and eventually, the wound becomes so infected that medical attention is needed. In the natural, we are never forced to go to a doctor. They don't invite themselves to our houses and force their way in. God never forces His way in. We have to seek Him out and ask for healing. God doesn't want our inner wounds from our past to fester. The good news

Chapter 13: Glorious Reflections

is that our heavenly Father wants to help us face what we can't face alone. He wants to heal us from our past. He doesn't want us to keep burying the brokenness inside of us. We were created to be whole in spirit, soul, and body.

Quiz or a Test?

Remember in school when your teacher said, "Take out your pencil, you have a quiz today"? Yikes! From what I remember, quizzes were usually unannounced. Quizzes were like "mini" tests.

You could look at your daily life like taking a quiz every day. You reflect on your daily happenings and think about how you can make things better or how awesome something worked.

I think it's very important to note here that we do not become "sin conscious" as we are allowing the Lord to perfect us. As we go through the transformation process of becoming like Jesus, we begin to look within ourselves, and things that we used to strive for become like second nature. Jesus never strived to be like His Father. Everything He did was what He saw His Father doing—it came naturally to Him without thinking about it.

When we reflect on our lives every day, we are looking to our Father to see what He's doing. Doing this helps prepare us for the "big test." Tests are like the final exam. We've learned everything in the unit and are ready to show what we know. We can look at a unit like a season in our lives. Everyone goes through seasons or transitions. When we are walking in the will of God, we become aware of the seasons and how to journey through them.

> Beloved, do not think it strange concerning the fiery trial which is to try you, as though some strange thing happened to you; but rejoice to the extent that you partake of Christ's sufferings, that when His glory is revealed, you may also be glad with exceeding joy. (1 Peter 4:12-13)

When we reflect on things in our lives, we are learning from our experiences. We have the best teacher ever! He is so patient and loving toward us. He wants the best for us so we can walk into the fullness of who He created us to be. In His eyes, we can never fail. He will keep giving us the test repeatedly until we can see what needs to be changed or learn what He wants to teach us. When we pass the test, we are propelled forward closer to our destiny. As I said before, He will never force anything on us. We have to want to go through the testing to move forward.

Relationship is the Key to Glorious Reflections

How do you view your relationship with your heavenly Father? I want you to take a moment and reflect on that question. Be honest here. His desire is for us to be in relationship with Him every day of the week, not just on Sundays. He loves it when we abide in Him, study His Word, and worship Him throughout the day. Day in, day out, Jesus should be the center of our lives. Our relationship with Him is the most important one we will ever have. He is our all-sufficient King. We should be taking every cry to Him. We should learn what it means to have a broken heart and contrite spirit.

> *The righteous* cry out, and the Lord hears, And delivers them out of all their troubles. The Lord *is* near to those who have a broken heart, And saves such as have a contrite spirit. Many *are* the afflictions of the righteous, But the Lord delivers him out of them all. (Psalm 34:17-19)

We were created for relationship, not only with our heavenly Father but with others as well. Most people who have an incredible relationship with God have learned to love people and that relationships should be two-sided, not just one. There's give and take. It's a partnership; two working together. They see others through the eyes of Jesus. Our relationships can be a reflection of who we are. When we see ourselves the way our Papa sees ourselves, we know who we are in Christ Jesus.

CHAPTER 13: GLORIOUS REFLECTIONS

We know we are sons and daughters of a king. Reflecting on our personal relationships will help our own reflections become glorious.

Below are a few examples of important relationships we all experience at one point or another. The key to resembling a glorious reflection is when we reflect on our relationships with others as well as with our loving Father. When we reflect on our personal relationships, we should be thinking about how we are representing our King Jesus.

Love Thy Neighbor

We've all been there at one time or another—having a hard time with loving someone around us. Now, I'm not just talking about people in our neighborhoods. There is always that one person who sticks out. You know what I'm talking about. In our workplace, church, community circles, and yes, even our neighborhoods. These are the people who rub you the wrong way. I've been there. When we see them coming, we want to disappear. It's easier to turn around and run rather than listen to them tell the same story we heard last week. Now hear me out. We need to learn to be more intentional and go out of our way to be in a relationship with people. I know this can be difficult for some people as it was for me.

I had a difficult time being around people because I like to be alone. Yup! I am a loner. I like to be by myself. Don't get me wrong—I like to fellowship with people. When I am in fellowship with others, my focus is usually on the kingdom. It is the only thing that I really like to talk about!

So why is it important to develop relationships with your neighbors or the people close to you? Because WHO is inside of you can make a difference in others. People will be drawn to you and want to be around you because of what you carry. They will want what you have—share it with them!

Step out in faith. God may have placed people in your path for a reason. Be intentional in reaching out to others. I'm not saying you have to have dinner dates to get super close to them, but just be there for them.

Let them know you're available to talk. You never know what God has planned. The reflection in you can change someone's life forever!

> Behold, how good and how pleasant *it is* for brethren to dwell together in unity! (Psalm 133:1)

Family Ties

Like our neighbors, there is always that one family member that everyone talks about—the "black sheep" of the family. They don't fall in line with the rest and, for some reason, are always making a scene. They may be rebellious, loud, angry, arrogant, confrontational, withdrawn—I could go on and on. Either way, they have a difficult time being in a family relationship. So, where do you come in? How can we strengthen our relationship with God if we can't adjust our thought patterns and our ways toward our loved ones?

We must be intentional about going out of our way and correcting some issues if need be. Sometimes it just takes a little love or an act of kindness to open the door. They may feel rejected or abandoned in some way. There may be bitterness or unforgiveness that is blocking them from allowing anyone into their life. I dare you to call someone in your family who has done you wrong and just love on them. Ask for their forgiveness. Give them an encouraging word. It will make all the difference, not only for them but for you as well. Is there someone in your family who is crying out? Are you listening? Is there someone God has placed on your heart? What are you waiting for? It's time to shine, and it begins within the walls of our own life. Be the light that people are drawn to. Let the light within you reflect on others.

> Bearing with one another, and forgiving one another, if anyone has a complaint against another; even as Christ forgave you, so you also *must do*. (Colossians 3:13)

Chapter 13: Glorious Reflections

Parenting 101

This is for the parents. I'm talking about your precious bundles of joy. You know, those cute little people who never talk back and do everything you ask them to do. Well, for some of you, that may be true. For others, not so much.

My wife and I have a couple of drama queens who are a little over the top sometimes. Now don't get me wrong. I love my children with all my heart, but let's face it, parenting isn't easy. When our children arrive, they don't come with a manual. It's easy to listen to other parents give advice or read a book on child-rearing. But not all children are the same. What works for one doesn't work for the other. For instance, it's not unusual that one child keeps their room spotless, and with the other you can't find the floor some days. Or how about keeping the kitchen clean? Don't even get me started on that one!

Yes, parenting can be difficult. But as I reflected on myself when I was young, I wasn't the neatest or cleanest kid either. In fact, there were times when I didn't want to listen to my parents, and I thought I knew it all. Yes, teenagers claim to already know everything there is to know about life. Remember arguing with your parents because they didn't know anything? I hear it from my kids all the time. They say, "Dad, it's so different than when you were a kid—you don't understand!" To be honest, it is different for our children in today's society. There's so much going against them that we need to be cheering them on. They have so much pressure from all sides. Kids are growing up more quickly than you or I did. The exposure to social media and the Internet are growing our kids up so much faster than we would like them to. Yes, we do our best to shield and protect them, but eventually, they have to grow up. That's where we come in as parents and do the best we can in this crazy world.

> And you, fathers, do not provoke your children to wrath, but bring them up in the training and admonition of the Lord. (Ephesians 6:4)

The King's Bridal Company

As with all children, they can upset or disappoint us. It's part of growing up and learning. When that happens, we can sometimes react without thinking. We've all been there as parents. We've blown up, overreacted, made them cry, or disappointed them. I know one thing for sure. My Lord doesn't flip out on me when I make a mistake. Does He get disappointed sometimes? Probably. Will He give up on me, call me a failure, tell me why can't I be perfect like Him? Never! He never will disappoint me. He continues to love me even through my mistakes and hardships. He is there for me, guiding me every step of the way. That's how we should be as parents. We should love our children to life, not to death.

Our children need to be disciplined, but with love, not anger. Children need to learn from their mistakes. How can they learn if we continue to tell them they did wrong without explaining to them the way they should go? Discipline should be done with the right attitude and with good character. Remember, our children will become parents themselves one day. We're not only their parents but their teachers. We are teaching them how to eventually be good parents.

When we speak to our children, we should be speaking words that will transform their lives. Let them know they have a destiny waiting for them and were created to be world changers. They are our children, but they are also children of God. Jesus would be encouraging them and loving them every step of the way.

One more thing I want to mention here. Just because our children leave the nest to walk out into the big world doesn't mean we stop being their parents. We still need to be their encouragers—even when they fall short of our expectations. Let them know that you're still rooting them on, right alongside Jesus. They will always be our babies, but they will always be His children. We want the best for our children, and so does He!

> Behold, children *are* a heritage from the Lord, the fruit of the womb *is* a reward. (Psalm 127:3)

CHAPTER 13: GLORIOUS REFLECTIONS

Spousal Support

Marital bliss, there's nothing like it. When two people are in unity and happily in love, life seems to flow endlessly. Sometimes marriage takes work. As we grow older together and things change, we need to learn to adjust. We suddenly get a "new family," and people we never knew before are now family, whether we like it or not. Adding children to the mix totally changes the dynamics of the relationship. It's not just "you and me" anymore. Now there's another human being who becomes our responsibility and needs lots of attention. It becomes "that was then, this is now" syndrome.

No matter what your relationship with your spouse looks like—newly married, empty nesters, blended family—one thing is for certain: putting God first is the key to a successful marriage.

I want to speak to the men for a bit (Ladies, this will be a good read for you too). There's an alarm ringing, and many men are sleeping right through it. You've gotten so used to the mundane sounds of life that you can't hear the alarm within you trying to shake you awake. You live day in, day out, doing what you can to be the best husband possible. Maybe you don't have the best marriage or you feel you need a little help. Or maybe you feel as though you have the perfect marriage and like things just how they are. Let me ask you something first, do you love your wife as Christ loves the church? Let's take a look at Ephesians 5:22-33 about husbands and wives:

> Wives, submit to your own husbands, as to the Lord. For the husband is head of the wife, as also Christ is head of the church; and He is the Savior of the body. Therefore, just as the church is subject to Christ, so *let* the wives *be* to their own husbands in everything.
>
> Husbands, love your wives, just as Christ also loved the church and gave Himself for her, that He might sanctify and cleanse her with the washing of water by the word, that He might present her to Himself a glorious church,

not having spot or wrinkle or any such thing, but that she should be holy and without blemish. So husbands ought to love their own wives as their own bodies; he who loves his wife loves himself. For no one ever hated his own flesh, but nourishes and cherishes it, just as the Lord *does* the church. For we are members of His body, of His flesh and of His bones. "For this reason a man shall leave his father and mother and be joined to his wife, and the two shall become one flesh." This is a great mystery, but I speak concerning Christ and the church. Nevertheless let each one of you in particular so love his own wife as himself, and let the wife *see* that she respects *her* husband. (Ephesians 5:22-33)

The first verse is a major one that some men have a big problem with. They get upset and wonder why their wives have no respect for them. In some marriages, men expect their wives to obey them as if they are the king of the castle. Guess what? God didn't make us men to be kings of the castle. Let's look specifically at verse 25. The scripture says that we ought to love our wives as Christ loves the church. I told my wife that if I didn't represent Christlike character and nature, then she did not have to submit to me. How can we expect our wives to submit to us if we act like selfish, foolish men who misrepresent who Christ truly is? I don't know about you, but my wife is everything to me. She's my lover and my friend. She is my partner in life. She is a part of me.

I had an encounter where the Lord showed me how special my relationship with my wife is and also revealed how important it is to be in one accord with each other. I was lying in bed early one morning, and I was in the spirit. All of a sudden, I felt something strange stirring within me. I suddenly saw my spirit go into my wife's spirit and unite as one. It was the most intense feeling I have ever felt. It was so beautiful that I could not even begin to describe the wonder of it. One thing is for sure. I truly understand what it means to be in unity with my wife. Philippians 2:2 (ESV) says, "Complete my joy by being of the same mind, having the same love, being in full accord and of one mind." There's no greater

Chapter 13: Glorious Reflections

joy for Him than for a husband and wife to be completely joined together in one flesh, one spirit, and one mind.

Husbands, take care of your wives. Wives, take care of your husbands. Pay attention to each other. Listen to each other. Appreciate each other. Be there for each other. Comfort each other. Always remember that marriage was given to us as a gift by God. Think about that for a minute. What a wondrous gift! When you're living out a godly marriage in the presence of God, you will benefit from all He wants to give you. Marriage is a partnership; you're in this together.

Times will get tough. No one said it would be easy. Whether you are a husband or a wife, you need to get out of your own way and let Jesus be the center of your relationship. When our eyes are focused on Him, He will lead us and guide us in the direction we should go—together as one. We need to support our spouses and pray *for* each other as well as *with* each other.

> **It's okay to be wrong and admit it. Believe it or not, your spouse will respect and honor you more.**

One last thing. At the end of the day, it doesn't matter who was right or wrong. Husbands and wives should be walking in unity. Sometimes it's better to just let it go and move on. For myself, I actually like to be wrong. I know that sounds crazy, but hear me out. When I'm wrong, the Lord always shows me I'm wrong. When that happens, it becomes a teachable moment. There's no way He is ever wrong, so when He tells me I made a mistake, I stop and listen. I'm learning that character and nature is so important. Being wrong builds integrity when we admit we made a mistake. It's okay to be wrong and admit it. Believe it or not, your spouse will respect and honor you more.

As we reflect on our relationships, it is imperative to remind you that the most important relationship we will ever have is with our heavenly

Father. As long as we put Him first above all others, the relationships that we cultivate with our family members, friends, co-workers, or acquaintances will always prosper in love. Once we start reflecting the King inside of us, our lives will begin to look and feel glorious. The atmosphere we carry will draw those around us to want what we have, and we start to become a glorious reflection of King Jesus.

The Return

We've looked at ourselves and our relationships with others, now let's think about something very important in our reflection of King Jesus. We've all thought about it at one time or another —the return of our King. Maybe it scares you a little, or maybe it excites you. Either way, you think to yourself, *Am I ready? What if He came back right this very second?*

> Now may the God of peace Himself sanctify you completely; and may your whole spirit, soul, and body be preserved blameless at the coming of our Lord Jesus Christ. (1 Thessalonians 5:23)

Ever since you were a little child or somewhere in your BC (before Christ) days, you most likely heard about the return of Christ. After being saved, we all go through some type of eye-opening awareness of Jesus Christ being our Lord and Savior. I know for me, it was the only thing on my lips. I was so excited to share the good news of Jesus Christ and what He did for me.

As I began to grow in Him, I would hear about His return—in the twinkling of an eye, I would meet Him in the sky (the rapture). I'm not here to argue about how or when it is going to happen—whether you are a pre-trib, mid-trib, or post-trib believer, I'm not going there. For the sake of having this discussion, it doesn't matter where you stand because regardless of your eschatological belief about the event, we all have common ground. We all believe that Jesus Christ is coming back for His glorious bride.

CHAPTER 13: GLORIOUS REFLECTIONS

Let's reflect here a little bit. Ask yourself if your belief is stopping you from becoming an intimate lover of the King. Are you busy trying to prove your doctrine about the timing of His return, or are you living desperate for His return? I think about it all the time. What will it be like? What will it be like to see Him—look into His eyes, see His gaze on me? What will it be like to talk with Him and hear His voice? What will it be like to hug Him and smell His fragrance?

Stop for a moment and just think about that. What would it be like for you? Right at this moment, I am seeing Him sitting on the edge of my bed watching me write this book with a big smile on His face. I can feel His love radiating toward me. Jesus is so intrigued with us, and it's His desire to extend His glorious ways to us.

During times when I am so fascinated with Him, I will sometimes get taken on exhilarating, awesome rides from the Holy Spirit. I believe these times can be a form of rapture. These encounters cause my heart to wait in expectation of His next return. While I am waiting for His return, my hope is that I will be in constant communion and prayer with Him. He delights in us when we seek His face, which causes us to be delighted in Him too. He wants to give us the desires of our hearts.

> Delight yourself also in the Lord, and He shall give you
> the desires of your heart. (Psalm 37:4)

The Holy Spirit truly loves to give us these wonderful encounters. For me, I get drawn closer to Jesus through them. In these experiences, I talk with the Holy Spirit, and He directs my attention to King Jesus. One way or another, whether it's through the Word or a supernatural encounter, the Holy Spirit is always trying to help us to be conformed into the image of Christ. In Galatians 5:22-23, it tells us about the fruit of the Spirit.

> But the fruit of the Spirit is love, joy, peace, longsuffering, kindness, goodness, faithfulness, gentleness, self-control. Against such there is no law.

The King's Bridal Company

These fruit of the Spirit are virtues that are the true character of Jesus. Everything in this entire world was created to point us to Jesus. These are the qualities that every believer should strive for, which make a difference in the world around us because the fruit of our spirit, not our works, is what is a true reflection of our King Jesus.

What happens next? As we continue to walk out this season of reflections, our hearts dramatically change. The inward reflection causes our hearts to inch closer to a longing to be with Jesus forever. We are waiting in expectancy for our lover's return for His bride. While we wait, let me ask you a question, "Are you ready?"

Chapter 14: Here Comes the Bride

The Proposal

Everything is set in place. He's been planning this for a long time. The perfect ring has been chosen. Now it's time for Him to propose—to get down on one knee and look into our eyes and ask us to marry Him. The bride of Christ has made herself ready for marriage to the King of Kings.

> Let us rejoice and exalt him and give him glory, because the wedding celebration of the Lamb has come. And his bride has made herself ready. (Revelation 19:7 TPT)

As with any wedding, there is an invitation to be invited. Throughout Scripture, Jesus invites us to come to Him. John 7:37 tells us that "If anyone thirsts, let him come to Me and drink." Matthew 11:28 says, "Come to Me, all *you* who labor and are heavy laden, and I will give you rest." We are invited to accept Him into our lives as our Lord and Savior. This invitation offers everything we need. He is not only our Lord and Savior but our Deliverer. He is all we need.

As we continue to grow up into all things and allow the Spirit of God to do a work in us, something shifts within us. We now begin to ready ourselves for the return of Christ.

The King's Bridal Company

> Until we all attain to the unity of the faith and of the knowledge of the Son of God, to mature manhood, to the measure of the stature of the fullness of Christ, so that we may no longer be children, tossed to and fro by the waves and carried about by every wind of doctrine, by human cunning, by craftiness in deceitful schemes. Rather, speaking the truth in love, we are to grow up in every way into him who is the head, into Christ. (Ephesians 4:13-15 ESV)

We get to a place in our lives where our hearts long to be with Him. We want to be His bride. Now I am about to say something here that may shake things up for some of you. I believe that when we are born into the kingdom, we have initial salvation. But in my own opinion, I do not believe that salvation qualifies us to be a part of the Bridal Company. I believe that the bride comes out of the church, and those who want to mature and continue to grow up into all things can be a part of the Bridal Company. Again, this is my own opinion, and I won't get into my beliefs in this book. That may be for another time and another book.

Now let's get back to our Bridegroom. When the Lord sees that we have allowed Him to search our hearts, then He will see how much we wanted to pay the price to be His. At the end of this journey, we will truly understand what it means to be transformed into His character and nature. We have laid down our lives as He laid down His for us.

> By this we know love, because He laid down His life for us. And we also ought to lay down *our* lives for the brethren. (1 John 3:16)

You have gotten to a place where you finally understand what 1 Corinthians 13 looks like, not just what it says, but how to experience true love. It's falling in love at first sight. The greatest marriage celebration is about to take place!

Chapter 14: Here Comes the Bride

Getting Ready

Any wedding celebration takes great planning and preparation. So how do we ready ourselves for the Bridegroom? How do we prepare to marry the fairest of them all? Every bride wants her wedding to be perfect. As little girls, they dream about the wedding they will have someday.

My wife and I actually had a fairytale wedding. Before I met her, I told everyone that I was going to meet and marry my Cinderella. I knew when I saw her that she was my princess. My wife planned most of our wedding, and it was absolutely beautiful! I know one thing for sure—it took my breath away when I saw her in her wedding dress for the first time. That's how it will be when Jesus sees his bride. It will be glorious!

So now what? How do we prepare for the greatest wedding of all time? We need to be asking ourselves some very important questions. Do you feel that you are truly ready for the Bridegroom to return for you? Have you represented character and nature above all other things? What image and reflection will He see when He looks at you—will it be Him or you? Have you allowed God to search out your heart? Can you say you are willing to surrender yourself wholeheartedly to walk into the fullness of what God has for you? Remember, Jesus is coming back for a spotless bride. What will He see in you?

If you've ever been a part of a wedding, whether your own, a family member's, or friend's, then you know the excitement and anticipation between the bridegroom and the bride. They've planned and waited what seems like forever for this special day. They want everything to be just perfect. That's how it is for us with Jesus. We wait in anticipation and excitement for the day to come.

> For our citizenship is in heaven, from which we also eagerly wait for the Savior, the Lord Jesus Christ, who will transform our lowly body that it may be conformed to His glorious body, according to the working by which He is able even to subdue all things to Himself. (Philippians 3:20-21)

The King's Bridal Company

We've been planning and preparing our lives so we can be united with Jesus and live with Him forever in eternity. What will it be like when you see the Bridegroom for the first time? I know for me, I can only imagine the splendor and awe of Him—his heart burning with a passionate love for us. Take a moment and think about what it would be like if Jesus came back right this second. How would you react? What would you do? Would you be excited? Nervous? Full of love? I know one thing for sure—when that day comes, it will be beyond our wildest dreams. It will be spectacular!

> **Get yourself ready and keep the burning desire for your lover lit within you until He comes back for His glorious bride.**

But until that day comes, we can let Him love us over and over while we wait for Him to return. Make Him a part of everything you desire to do. Let Him lead you in every direction, and submit your entire being into His loving hands. Get yourself ready and keep the burning desire for your lover lit within you until He comes back for His glorious bride.

> Stay dressed for action and keep your lamps burning.
> (Luke 12:35 ESV)

Keeping the Candle Lit

Unfortunately, many marriages fail because there is a lack of unity within the marriage. For some, the "honeymoon" phase quickly dies out. They let the cares of this world fool them into believing that romance lasts forever because of money and material things. If we don't totally commit ourselves to love and a burning desire to keep the relationship going, then it can be easy to get sidetracked from our one true love. We

Chapter 14: Here Comes the Bride

easily forget the feeling of falling in love and having eyes only for our lover. The romance slowly slips away.

Our relationship with our heavenly Father is like a romance. We only have eyes for Him. We need to make time for only Him—our first true love. Colossians 3:2 tells us, "Set your mind on things above, not on things on the earth." In this romance between us and our One True Love, we need to remember to keep our gaze on HIM and not things of this world.

I've seen it happen to the best people. They give their lives over to Christ, and they're on a spiritual high. They want to learn everything there is to know about Jesus and will devote every second to growing and maturing in His ways. Then something happens. They lose the spark. The fire that was once burning bright and long starts to dim. They have allowed the cares of this earth to overtake their thoughts and actions. They start to put themselves first before putting the Lord first in their lives. Remember, it takes two to be in a relationship. He will always be there for us, but if we busy ourselves with matters of this world, our eyes and heart begin to wander. Nothing in this world should make us happier than being with Him. We need to keep the candle lit so the fire we have for Him will continue to grow and burn bright.

> Be enthusiastic to serve the Lord, keeping your passion toward him boiling hot! Radiate with the glow of the Holy Spirit and let him fill you with excitement as you serve him. (Romans 12:11 TPT)

How do we do this? We need to continually seek His face and put Him first above all things, even other relationships in our lives. When we do, everything will fall into place. We need to live in the Word of God, pray fervently in the Spirit, worship, and write love letters to our King. He only has eyes for us, and our eyes should be set on Him.

This season of life is the time to shine and keep the candle burning bright so others can see Him within us. Jesus Christ, the hope of glory who lives within us, eagerly desires to take us deeper than we could ever have imagined. We need to keep the fire burning! Let's occupy until He returns with great expectation of Him giving us more and more of His love.

Destiny Mirrors

As we continually grow into a desire to burn with fire toward our lover, the intense burning has started to create and shape our true destiny. What we once thought we understood about our destiny has become a thing of the past. As we have allowed the Lord to do a deep work within us, what we thought we knew about ourselves is no longer true. We begin to see the fullness of our destiny that He has been dreaming for us so we can walk into what *He* has planned for us, not what *we* have planned for ourselves.

> We have become his poetry, a re-created people that will fulfill the destiny he has given each of us, for we are joined to Jesus, the Anointed One. Even before we were born, God planned in advance *our destiny* and the good works we would do *to fulfill it*! (Ephesians 2:10 TPT)

The fire inside of us has started to transform us into looking like our King. What He is seeing is well-pleasing to His eyes and to others. What you have allowed yourself to mirror is the entire reason you were created. He chose you to become a mirror image of His Son Jesus before He formed the world. Father God also knows who the ones are who want to be conformed into the image of His Son before any human came into existence.

> For whom He foreknew, He also predestined *to be* conformed to the image of His Son, that He might be the firstborn among many brethren. Moreover whom He predestined, these He also called; whom He called, these He also justified; and whom He justified, these He also glorified. (Romans 8:29-30)

Chapter 14: Here Comes the Bride

One of the Greek definitions of the word *predestined* means to set the limits in advance. He already knew beforehand who would want to allow themselves to be pushed to the limit and pay a very steep price to be conformed into the image of His Son. Because He already knew this, He developed the specific course of life designed only for you that would help mature and develop you into the character and nature of King Jesus. There are very few who want to come to the end of themselves, lay down their entire lives, and allow Him to search out their inner being. The ones who are willing have begun to rewrite an entirely new chapter of their lives on destiny. They are learning that at the center of their destiny lies King Jesus.

> **A specific destiny has been designed especially for you. It is not a one-size-fits-all destiny for everyone.**

A specific destiny has been designed especially for you. It is not a one-size-fits-all destiny for everyone. Trust in the Lord and keep asking Him for His guidance along the way. There's no possible way to reach the fullness of your destiny without His help. And remember, Father God is cheering for you, along with the Great Cloud of Witnesses. You are never alone, so don't think you can do this on your own in your own strength. God will bring help along the way and counsel you when you need it.

The true body of Christ in its fullness has learned to mirror the character and nature of Jesus. We cannot forget that our individual ministries are part of a corporate end-time ministry and were never intended to be apart from the rest of the body of Christ. When the five-fold ministry is functioning correctly, the Corporate Bride mirrors the image of Christ. I will be discussing the importance of the five-fold ministry in my next book. When we are walking out our destiny, we need to remember that our training is not going to be like everyone else's. The Lord has chosen us to function uniquely in our own expressions.

> And He Himself gave some *to be* apostles, some prophets, some evangelists, and some pastors and teachers, for the equipping of the saints for the work of ministry, for the edifying of the body of Christ, till we all come to the unity of the faith and of the knowledge of the Son of God, to a perfect man, to the measure of the stature of the fullness of Christ. (Ephesians 4:11-13)

The five-fold ministry was given to the church to help us walk into greatness and teach us how to live in the full measure of character and nature. This is the most glorious reflection! Our destiny now starts to mirror the King. As long as we keep moving forward, we will not miss our mark.

Weight of His Glory

Have you ever been to a conference or service where the glory of the Lord is so powerful you feel His immense weight upon you? In my early years of hungering for more of the Lord, I decided to attend a conference and was able to experience that feeling for the first time in my life. I was surprised at the number of people waiting in line outside on that hot summer day. I got in line and began to wonder what all the hype was about. The doors finally opened, and the people flooded inside. As I walked through the doors, I immediately felt a change in the atmosphere. As the people entered, some began laughing and weeping uncontrollably. I thought to myself, "What's going on here?"

During worship, I decided to position myself a distance from everyone else so I could "check things out." Everyone looked like they were having so much fun with the Lord, and I wanted to experience this for myself. I closed my eyes and began to pray. Something so incredible came over me that I can't even explain it in words. I couldn't move any part of my body. I was so peaceful. The feeling I was experiencing was so intense and amazing at the same time. I opened my eyes, and, to my astonishment, I was staring at the ceiling! I don't even remember moving my body—how did I get on the floor?

Chapter 14: Here Comes the Bride

I was changed forever after that day. Now I understood why the people were so eager to get inside. They were waiting for Him, for His presence. Once you experience the weight of His glory, you can't get enough of it!

> So that the priests could not continue ministering because of the cloud; for the glory of the Lord filled the house of God. (2 Chronicles 5:14)

The glorious Bride is so mesmerized by His presence that nothing else matters in that moment. They can't get enough of His glory! The Bride wants the moment to last forever—they have learned to treasure every glorious moment with Him. There is a change that can take place during this precious time if you truly believe that He can work within you as you surrender yourself to Him.

The manifest presence of God trumps everything you thought you ever knew about Him. There's nothing like it on this present earth.

> Jesus said to her, "Did I not say to you that if you would believe you would see the glory of God?" (John 11:40)

The manifest presence of God trumps everything you thought you ever knew about Him. There's nothing like it on this present earth. When we get into His presence and learn to behold His glory, the weight of His glory will transform us into His image.

> But we all, with unveiled face, beholding as in a mirror the glory of the Lord, are being transformed into the same image from glory to glory, just as by the Spirit of the Lord. (2 Corinthians 3:18)

Never be in a hurry when you are with Him—learn to linger in His glory. Don't speak to Him—just rest in Him. When we linger in God's presence, it allows Him to reveal things to us. For example, Abraham spent a lot of time in the presence of God, and he didn't speak much; he just listened. In Genesis 18:17, the Lord said, "Shall I hide from Abraham what I am doing?" God was going to wipe out Sodom and Gomorrah, but because Abraham had learned to dwell in His presence, the Lord revealed His plans to Abraham so he could intercede. Had Abraham not lingered, the outcome for Lot might have been very different.

The Lord is looking for a presence-driven bride who loves to bask in His glory. He wants to share His most intimate secrets with her. We need to remember something—experiencing and resting in the heaviness of His glory is so amazing, but there is still more. We are called to take that glory among people. The Lord is looking for someone who will want to carry His glory.

Carriers of Glory

It is an amazing experience to witness the power of God when His presence is so electrifying that it can seem almost tangible. Some presence-driven people love it so much that they tend to be looked upon differently because all they want to do is soak and get drenched with love. I wish that was all we are required to do, but that's not the case. There is more than just going from event to event to get drunk in His Spirit. Yes, it feels incredible, and the feeling can last for days—sometimes even weeks—and we love it, but there is something we need to understand. When we receive His glory, it's not just for us, but to share with others also. As we draw near to God and receive what He has for us, we need to be asking Him for more. He wants us to ask for more of His glory because He will give us opportunities to share it for others to experience.

> But you shall receive power when the Holy Spirit has come upon you; and you shall be witnesses to Me in Jerusalem, and in all Judea and Samaria, and to the end of the earth. (Acts 1:8)

CHAPTER 14: HERE COMES THE BRIDE

We need to be asking for an overfilling of His Spirit so when people draw near to us, they feel the power of the One who created them emanating from us. The Lord will set people in our path, so they have every opportunity to find their destiny. What they see and feel will get them thinking about their own lives because they come face-to-face with Jesus through you. People need the power of God, and we should not only want to receive it but to carry His glory to others too.

There are some amazing glory carriers in our midst—what's their secret? It all goes back to one thing: relationship. These carriers of glory are cultivating a friendship with the Holy Spirit.

> Do you not know that you are the temple of God and *that* the Spirit of God dwells in you? If anyone defiles the temple of God, God will destroy him. For the temple of God is holy, which *temple* you are. (1 Corinthians 16-17)

The secret of living, breathing, and walking in a lifestyle of glory is having His Spirit within us. He uses us as vessels to be carriers of His glory. The power of God is demonstrated through us because He dwells within us. Why wouldn't we want to get to know the Spirit of the living God? He wants to get to know us, and longs for us to want to know more of Him. The Holy Spirit desires for us to have a deep-rooted relationship with Him.

Have you ever met someone for the first time and felt a sense that you just wanted to get to know that person better? I'm not talking about lust or love, but an attraction where your spirit is drawn to theirs. You can't explain it because you just met them, but you know instantly that you like them. You begin to develop a friendship, and before long, you're talking and hanging out more, and the next thing you know, you're best friends. In time, you feel comfortable enough to confide your deepest, darkest secrets—things that you cannot share with anyone else. It's a give-and-take relationship with each of you giving comfort, guidance, and support to one another. You can always count on this friend to be there for you. They are there when you need them most and will give you the hard truth in love whether you like it or not. That is how it is with the Holy Spirit. He wants to be your best friend.

The Holy Spirit is called the *paraclete* in the original Greek, which refers to Him being our helper. The Holy Spirit is a person—He feels, He senses, and He loves. We can hurt Him or grieve Him. He is sneaky (in a good way—always full of wonderful surprises) and is always on time. Most of all, He wants to empower us.

> And I will pray the Father, and He will give you another Helper, that He may abide with you forever—the Spirit of truth, whom the world cannot receive, because it neither sees Him nor knows Him; but you know Him, for He dwells with you and will be in you. I will not leave you orphans; I will come to you. (John 14-16-18)

So what is the Holy Spirit's intention other than wanting to be our friend? For starters, He wants to draw us closer to Jesus. He wants to take us into the things of God.

> But as it is written: "Eye has not seen, nor ear heard, nor have entered into the heart of man the things which God has prepared for those who love Him." But God has revealed them to us through His Spirit. For the Spirit searches all things, yes, the deep things of God. For what man knows the things of a man except the spirit of the man which is in him? Even so no one knows the things of God except the Spirit of God. (1 Corinthians 2:9-11)

The Holy Spirit knows the purpose of God, but He also knows the mind of God. He will always search us out and help us to understand the deeper things of God. Man cannot teach us to see and hear the deeper things of the Spirit. It doesn't matter how long we study; the things of the Spirit go beyond the intellectual mind and science. The Holy Spirit reveals where the deeper things dwell, and this comes out of intimacy with Him.

Chapter 14: Here Comes the Bride

Besides wanting to be our friend, the Holy Spirit also wants to purify and refine us. Allowing the Spirit of God to purify and refine us helps us with our spiritual well-being. Revelation 3:18 says, "I counsel you to buy from Me gold refined in the fire, that you may be rich; and white garments, that you may be clothed, *that* the shame of your nakedness may not be revealed; and anoint your eyes with eye salve, that you may see." If we can get rid of the "junk in our trunk," then we can come to the end of ourselves and start to see from a heavenly perspective.

> **Carriers of His glory have such a friendship with the Spirit of God that He becomes part of everything they do in life.**

Carriers of His glory have such a friendship with the Spirit of God that He becomes part of everything they do in life. Every thought or action is shared with the Holy Spirit. It is like a companion that never leaves. You don't want to make any decision without Him because you know He will be there to guide you in the right direction. The Bridal Company will be a people who never exclude their best friend from anything. They have a reverence for Him and have learned to live their life in awe of their precious, beloved Holy Spirit by abiding in His presence.

The Awe of God

Take a moment and look around you. Wherever you are right now, look outside your window and see how amazing our God is. For me, He is everywhere I look. I am in awe just thinking about all He created. There are many natural wonders in our world that take my breath away because of the beauty of His handiwork. Every detail was planned when He created the heavens and the earth. In moments like that, I just want to worship Him and give Him all the glory, honor, and praise.

THE KING'S BRIDAL COMPANY

When we look around and think about how awesome our God is, sometimes we forget to think about things beyond our natural realm of seeing—His angels. Psalm 91:11 tells us, "For He shall give His angels charge over you, to keep you in all your ways." Isn't that incredible? We need to keep in mind that we are not to worship or glorify angels, but I am in awe that He cared enough for me to send His angels to watch over me. I have had numerous encounters with these amazing messengers of God.

There are times during an encounter I have with Him when the reverential fear of the Lord is so intense that I am in shock and awe of Him. When He comes and just touches me or when the Holy Spirit catches me up, I am completely undone with His awesomeness.

> Let all the earth fear the Lord; Let all the inhabitants of the world stand in awe of Him. (Psalm 33:8)

Have you ever closed your eyes and imagined the Father looking at you? What do you see? I am most certain that He is looking adoringly at you with all the love He has for you. Think about His goodness and what He's done for you. He sent His Son to die for you—the ultimate sacrifice!

> For God so loved the world that He gave His only begotten Son, that whoever believes in Him should not perish but have everlasting life. (John 3:16)

He is a loving, Holy God, majestic in all His ways and brilliant beyond anything we could imagine. His glory covers all the earth. We are witnesses of His splendor. We cannot forget about the awe of Him. Sometimes we put all our focus on other things, and we start to forget about the wonder of Him. I think this is important to remember because it will keep us grounded in Him and create a balance in our lives. It's okay to think about saving souls, assignments, giftings, mantles, the end times, and church or *ekklesia*. We *should* be thinking about these things. But there are pastors or evangelists who tend to get caught up in their own ministries that they forget about who He is rather than what He can do. Again, these things are important, but we must remain focused on the

Chapter 14: Here Comes the Bride

wonder of who He is because once we put our focus on Him, everything else will fall into place.

> Now therefore, if you will indeed obey My voice and keep My covenant, then you shall be a special treasure to Me above all people; for all the earth is Mine. (Exodus 19:5)

The Bridal Company has learned to capture and sustain the awe of God. They haven't forgotten their first love. They truly understand the mystery of Christ living within them, manifesting His glory through them. The Bridal Company is in reverential wonder that their lover is coming for them. They anticipate His return and are actively waiting in awe.

Some years had gone by since my first heavenly encounter with the golden city, and there I was, caught up again by the Holy Spirit, circling this beautiful city of gold. It was just like I remembered from the last time the Lord brought me to visit—still as marvelous and full of splendor. Once again, I was in complete awe of what I was seeing. The radiance of the city was so breathtaking. I thought to myself, *Why am I always above it, looking down instead of below it, looking up?* His answer to me was, "Sal, the ones who will enter this city are the ones who are willing to go lower."

If the way in is down, then we must learn to go low. Our lives must represent humility, being poor in spirit, having meekness, and being pure in heart. Learn to "be the attitude" (Beatitudes) and desire to be conformed into the image of His Son, Jesus. It is His desire to give you this city. You have arrived!

> Then I, John, saw the holy city, New Jerusalem, coming down out of heaven from God, prepared as a bride adorned for her husband. (Revelation 21:2)

To Be Continued…

About the Author

Sal Cerra's life and ministry is marked by supernatural experiences with God, visions, revelations, and visitations. Having been through fiery trials throughout his life, both Sal and his wife, Kristine, are living testimonies of God's promise of restoration. Together they founded Destiny Fire Ministries and have a heart for seeing people set free from bondage and past struggles. Their desire is for people to see themselves for who they really are—true sons and daughters of a loving heavenly Father, able to walk in the fullness they were created for, which will cultivate the deep intimacy with God that every believer can have.

Since Sal first began walking with God, his deepest longing has been to understand what genuine intimacy and true sonship really looks like. Through his years in business and ministry, this desire for intimacy with God has led him in a desperate pursuit of the Father's heart. The focus of Sal's message is to help people know who the Father really is, which leads to them falling in love with Jesus, experiencing levels of God's grace, and discovering their true identity as sons and daughters of God.

Sal was not only involved with his family's business for twenty-five years, but had also owned his own construction business for twenty years concurrently. He completed four years of schooling about ministry and the supernatural. Sal and Kristine have six children and one grandchild, and live in central Florida. Sal can be contacted at destiny@destinyfire.org or from his website: www.destinyfire.org.

Other books by Sal Cerra

Within the pages of this book awaits something that has been crying out for you your entire lifetime. It is the cry of purpose—the reason you were created. It's been there throughout your existence and before you were ever born. The Father's ultimate design for your life has been uniquely crafted together, but is often overlooked because of this world's system.

Destiny Dreams reveals the truths that not only does a destiny exist for you, but it is actually dreaming and working toward cultivating an incredible relationship with our heavenly Father. Discover unimaginable experiences and expectations that you never thought possible. Your destiny is calling out to you!

Find out more at www.destinyfire.org.

www.ingramcontent.com/pod-product-compliance
Lightning Source LLC
Chambersburg PA
CBHW072000070526
44583CB00015B/1274